Azure IoT Development Cookbook

Develop and manage robust IoT solutions

Yatish Patil

BIRMINGHAM - MUMBAI

Azure IoT Development Cookbook

First published: August 2017

Production reference: 1100817

Published by Packt Publishing Ltd.
Livery Place
35 Livery Street
Birmingham
B3 2PB, UK.

ISBN 978-1-78728-300-8

www.packtpub.com

Credits

Author
Yatish Patil

Reviewers
Ruben Oliva Ramos
Roberto Freato

Acquisition Editor
Heramb Bhavsar

Content Development Editor
Devika Battike

Technical Editor
Prachi Sawant

Production Coordinator
Aparna Bhagat

Copy Editor
Juliana Nair

Project Coordinator
Judie Jose

Proofreader
Safis Editing

Indexer
Aishwarya Gangawane

Graphics
Kirk D'Penha

About the Author

Yatish Patil is currently working with Saviant Consulting as a technical project manager. He has delivered enterprise IoT and analytics applications using Microsoft Azure, ASP.NET, MVC, C#, SQL Server, and NoSQL. He has diverse industrial experience in IT and has worked in a variety of domains, such as utilities, manufacturing, and engineering.

He has completed his certification in Developing Azure Solutions in the Microsoft Azure Certification.

Yatish was also the technical reviewer for a Microsoft Azure-based technology book *Microsoft Azure IaaS Essentials*, which teaches guides Microsoft Azure subscribers how to design, configure, and build cloud-based infrastructure using Microsoft Azure.

Yatish was among the industry speakers at India IoT Symposium, 2016. He delivered the industry session on remote asset monitoring with Microsoft Azure IoT Suite.

I would like to thank my father, mother, and brother for always being supportive and letting me do what I want; my wife, Vasudha, and my son, Rudra, for tolerating the many late nights it took to write this book.

I would like to thank my mentors, who have been instrumental in my career - Anubhav Dwivedi, CEO Saviant, and Sujit Karpe, CTO Saviant, for being wonderful teachers, bosses, leaders, and friends, for providing me opportunities and encouraging me, and making me a proud member of Team Saviant, a workplace for inspiration, continuous innovation, and growth.

Last but not least, I thank the entire team at Packt, especially Heramb Bhavsar, Devika Battike, Prachi Sawant, and the reviewers, for their patience, suggestions, and support throughout this project and making this a memorable project for me.

About the Reviewers

Roberto Freato has been an independent IT consultant since he started to work. Working for small software factories while he was studying, after his MSc in computer science engineering with a thesis about consumer cloud computing he got specialization in Cloud and Azure. Today he works as a freelance consultant for major companies in Italy, helping clients to design and kick-off their distributed software solutions. He trains for the developer community in the free time, speaking in many conferences. He is a Microsoft MVP since 2010.

Ruben Oliva Ramos is a computer systems engineer from Tecnologico of Leon Institute, with a master's degree in computer and electronic systems engineering, teleinformatics and networking specialization from University of Salle Bajio in Leon, Guanajuato Mexico. He has more than 5 years of experience in developing WEB applications to control and monitor devices connected with Arduino and Raspberry Pi using WEB Frameworks and Cloud Services to build the Internet of Things applications.

He is a mechatronics teacher at University of Salle Bajio and teaches students on the master's degree in design and engineering of mechatronics systems. He also works at Centro de Bachillerato Tecnologico Industrial 225 in Leon, Guanajuato Mexico, teaching subjects such as electronics, robotics and control, automation and microcontrollers at mechatronics technician career, consultant, and developer projects in areas such as monitoring systems and datalogger data using technologies such as Android, iOS, Windows Phone, HTML5, PHP, CSS, Ajax, JavaScript, Angular, and ASP .NET; databases such as SQlite, mongoDB, and MySQL; Web servers such as Node.js and IIS; and hardware programming such as Arduino, Raspberry pi, Ethernet Shield, GPS and GSM/GPRS, ESP8266, and control and monitor systems for Data Acquisition and Programming.

I would like to thank my savior and lord, Jesus Christ for giving me strength and courage to pursue this project, to my dearest wife, Mayte, our two lovely sons, Ruben and Dario, To my father (Ruben), my dearest mom (Rosalia), my brother (Juan Tomas), and my sister (Rosalia) whom I love, for all their support while reviewing this book, for allowing me to pursue my dream and tolerating not being with them after my busy day job.

www.PacktPub.com

For support files and downloads related to your book, please visit www.PacktPub.com.

Did you know that Packt offers eBook versions of every book published, with PDF and ePub files available? You can upgrade to the eBook version at www.PacktPub.com and as a print book customer, you are entitled to a discount on the eBook copy. Get in touch with us at service@packtpub.com for more details.

At www.PacktPub.com, you can also read a collection of free technical articles, sign up for a range of free newsletters and receive exclusive discounts and offers on Packt books and eBooks.

https://www.packtpub.com/mapt

Get the most in-demand software skills with Mapt. Mapt gives you full access to all Packt books and video courses, as well as industry-leading tools to help you plan your personal development and advance your career.

Why subscribe?

- Fully searchable across every book published by Packt
- Copy and paste, print, and bookmark content
- On demand and accessible via a web browser

Customer Feedback

Thanks for purchasing this Packt book. At Packt, quality is at the heart of our editorial process. To help us improve, please leave us an honest review on this book's Amazon page at `https://www.amazon.com/dp/1787283003`.

If you'd like to join our team of regular reviewers, you can e-mail us at `customerreviews@packtpub.com`. We award our regular reviewers with free eBooks and videos in exchange for their valuable feedback. Help us be relentless in improving our products!

Table of Contents

Preface

The Microsoft Azure Internet of Things (IoT) platform is a set of IoT capabilities enabling businesses to build and gain value from IoT solutions quickly and efficiently. As part of their IoT Suite, Microsoft Azure IoT services enable the customers in their IoT journey - whether they are on their journey or looking to scale their IoT solutions, transforming their digital business.

Today, developers are leveraging the power of IoT in building IoT solutions for enterprises by getting started quickly with help from Azure IoT services - a set of open source SDKs, samples, pre-configured solutions, and tools provided by Microsoft Azure.

Azure IoT Hub is an easy and secure way to connect, provision, and manage millions of IoT devices, which are continuously sending and receiving billions of messages per specified or configurable interval. IoT Hub helps the communication between IoT devices and their solutions in the cloud, allowing them to store, analyze, alert, and take action on that data in real time. IoT Hub provides secure, reliable, two-way communication - both device-to-cloud and cloud-to-device - over open protocols such as MQTT, HTTPS, and AMQPS that are commonly used in IoT scenarios.

The aim of this book is to help the developer who wants to connect devices to IoT Hub, manage the IoT Hub service itself, and integrate IoT Hub into their overall IoT solution in the cloud. It discusses how to implement secure IoT solution, and implement IoT analytics scenarios. It also dives into pre-configured solutions, followed by some real device connectivity to explore the capabilities of IoT Hub.

What this book covers

Chapter 1, *Getting Started with the Azure IoT Platform*, introduces the Microsoft Azure IoT platform, which provides device management capabilities, as well as secure and bidirectional communication between millions of devices. Azure IoT Hub is the key for building IoT solutions. The chapter will focus on the different ways to create an IoT Hub service to connect devices. It will also dive more into the Azure IoT SDK and how the pricing works for Azure IoT Hub.

Chapter 2, *Introducing Device Management*, explains that a crucial part of IoT is to manage the device. Azure IoT Hub provides standard device management capabilities. With this feature synchronization between devices, updating metadata and executing actions are easy to implement for a developer. This chapter's focus will be to explain how to do device management with Azure IoT Hub, device communication operation, update device metadata, and execute commands.

Chapter 3, *IoT Hub Messaging and Commands*, describes the secure messaging between the connected device and IoT Hub. The chapter shows how to send an IoT device-to-cloud messages and receive cloud-to-device messages. It also shows how to ingest the file by uploading it to storage and updating device firmware remotely.

Chapter 4, *Azure IoT Communication Protocols*, focuses on the way IoT devices communicates with the cloud using various protocols. We will look at different recipes that show the different communication protocols IoT Hub supports and how we can connect these IoT devices to IoT Hub.

Chapter 5, *Azure IoT Hub Security and Best Practices*, dives more into IoT Hub concept such as securing and following best security practices. This chapter covers the different security standard supported by IoT Hub and how your IoT solution can make use of them to build a secure platform for connected devices.

Chapter 6, *IoT Suite and Pre-Configured Solutions*, discusses building common IoT scenarios quickly and going live with these solutions. Microsoft Azure IoT Suite is IoT Hub with a combination of commonly used cloud services such as storage, stream analytics, and visualizations using Power BI. It provides an example for each plugin by highlighting the requirements for each setup.

Chapter 7, *Azure IoT Analytics*, discusses the Azure services, which in conjunction with IoT Hub help businesses to drive their objectives. With connected devices, some significant challenges are seen with the diverse data volume and variety. This chapter covers the different Azure analytics services, that works with IoT Hub and help businesses to achieve their outcomes.

Chapter 8, *Using Real Devices to Connect and Implement Azure IoT Hub*, discusses how to configure and connect a real device with IoT Hub. This chapter covers a real-world case study and shows how it can be solved with IoT. We will discusses about reference IoT architecture, which can be built on top of the Azure platform. It also covers also connecting a Raspberry Pi device to implement a solution such as smart parking.

Chapter 9, *Managing the Azure IoT Hub*, dives more into the ways to manage the IoT Hub service with different tools and techniques. It starts with using the device explorer to manage the capabilities of IoT Hub, and moves onto getting diagnostic information using the Azure portal for the operational logs and metrics, which provides detailed logging of connected devices, and shows how to find solutions using debugging tools and hands-on tips.

What you need for this book

This book assumes a basic level of complete with the Microsoft Azure platform, basic knowledge of cloud computing, and knowledge of how to implement a solution on Microsoft Azure. The book will go through a IoT Hub setup on the Azure environment, which may require an understanding of C# and cloud concepts. If you have experience of Microsoft Azure Services, this is an advantage. We will be covering both the IoT services and IoT device client sides with open source SDKs from Azure IoT.

Azure IoT SDK supports C, .NET, Java, and Node.js-based development. However, this book requires that you have experience with C# and .NET.

The minimum hardware requirements are as follows:

- CPU: 4 cores
- Memory: 8 GB RAM
- Disk space: 80 GB

In this book, you will need the following software list:

- Visual Studio 2015
- Latest Azure SDK
- Microsoft Azure Account

Internet connectivity is required to install the necessary .NET packages and the Azure IoT SDK.

Who this book is for

This book focuses on providing essential information about the theory and application of Azure IoT Hub techniques and their applications within the context of Azure IoT development. The book is targeted towards both IoT hobbyist's developers and IT professionals who are new to Azure IoT and Microsoft Azure IoT platform. Azure IoT makes it just as approachable for a novice as a seasoned professional, helping you quickly be productive and on your way towards creating and testing IoT solutions.

For fast reading on the major components from the Microsoft Azure documentation at `http
s://docs.microsoft.com/en-gb/azure/`. This covers the latest updates on Azure platform releases. This book is essentially intended for IoT developers, big data architects, cloud developers, and .NET engineers. If you are also willing to build your IoT solution on top of the Azure platform, then this book is ideal for you. If you already have a running IoT solution, this book can help to speed up with the use of IoT Hub and IoT Suite in a fast-paced way.

Sections

In this book, you will find several headings that appear frequently (Getting ready, How to do it, How it works, There's more, and See also).

To give clear instructions on how to complete a recipe, we use these sections as follows:

Getting ready

This section tells you what to expect in the recipe, and describes how to set up any software or any preliminary settings required for the recipe.

How to do it...

This section contains the steps required to follow the recipe.

How it works...

This section usually consists of a detailed explanation of what happened in the previous section.

There's more...

This section consists of additional information about the recipe in order to make the reader more knowledgeable about the recipe.

See also

This section provides helpful links to other useful information for the recipe.

Conventions

In this book, you will find a number of styles of text that distinguish between different kinds of information. Here are some examples of these styles, and an explanation of their meaning.

Code words in text, database table names, folder names, filenames, file extensions, pathnames, dummy URLs, user input, and Twitter handles are shown as follows:" Retrieve the device identity by `deviceId`."

A block of code is set as follows:

```
try
{
device = await registryManager.GetDeviceAsync(deviceId);
}
```

Any command-line input or output is written as follows:

```
git clone https://github.com/Azure/iot-edge.git
```

New terms and **important** words are shown in bold. Words that you see on the screen, in menus or dialog boxes for example, appear in the text like this: "Select **Set up a new device**."

Warnings or important notes appear in a box like this.

Tips and tricks appear like this.

Reader feedback

Feedback from our readers is always welcome. Let us know what you think about this book-what you liked or disliked. Reader feedback is important for us as it helps us develop titles that you will really get the most out of.

To send us general feedback, simply e-mail feedback@packtpub.com, and mention the book's title in the subject of your message.

If there is a topic that you have expertise in and you are interested in either writing or contributing to a book, see our author guide at www.packtpub.com/authors.

Customer support

Now that you are the proud owner of a Packt book, we have a number of things to help you to get the most from your purchase.

Downloading the example code

You can download the example code files for this book from your account at http://www.packtpub.com. If you purchased this book elsewhere, you can visit http://www.packtpub.com/support and register to have the files e-mailed directly to you.

You can download the code files by following these steps:

1. Log in or register to our website using your e-mail address and password.
2. Hover the mouse pointer on the **SUPPORT** tab at the top.
3. Click on **Code Downloads & Errata**.
4. Enter the name of the book in the **Search** box.
5. Select the book for which you're looking to download the code files.
6. Choose from the drop-down menu where you purchased this book from.
7. Click on **Code Download**.

You can also download the code files by clicking on the **Code Files** button on the book's webpage at the Packt Publishing website. This page can be accessed by entering the book's name in the **Search** box. Please note that you need to be logged in to your Packt account.

Once the file is downloaded, please make sure that you unzip or extract the folder using the latest version of:

- WinRAR / 7-Zip for Windows
- Zipeg / iZip / UnRarX for Mac
- 7-Zip / PeaZip for Linux

The code bundle for the book is also hosted on GitHub at `https://github.com/PacktPublishing/Azure-IoT-Development-Cookbook`. We also have other code bundles from our rich catalog of books and videos available at `https://github.com/PacktPublishing/`. Check them out!

Downloading the color images of this book

We also provide you with a PDF file that has color images of the screenshots/diagrams used in this book. The color images will help you better understand the changes in the output. You can download this file from `https://www.packtpub.com/sites/default/files/downloads/AzureIoTDevelopmentCookbook_ColorImages.pdf`.

Errata

Although we have taken every care to ensure the accuracy of our content, mistakes do happen. If you find a mistake in one of our books-maybe a mistake in the text or the code-we would be grateful if you could report this to us. By doing so, you can save other readers from frustration and help us improve subsequent versions of this book. If you find any errata, please report them by visiting `http://www.packtpub.com/submit-errata`, selecting your book, clicking on the **Errata Submission Form** link, and entering the details of your errata. Once your errata are verified, your submission will be accepted and the errata will be uploaded to our website or added to any list of existing errata under the Errata section of that title.

To view the previously submitted errata, go to `https://www.packtpub.com/books/content/support` and enter the name of the book in the search field. The required information will appear under the **Errata** section.

Piracy

Piracy of copyrighted material on the internet is an ongoing problem across all media. At Packt, we take the protection of our copyright and licenses very seriously. If you come across any illegal copies of our works in any form on the internet, please provide us with the location address or website name immediately so that we can pursue a remedy.

Please contact us at `copyright@packtpub.com` with a link to the suspected pirated material.

We appreciate your help in protecting our authors and our ability to bring you valuable content.

Questions

If you have a problem with any aspect of this book, you can contact us at `questions@packtpub.com`, and we will do our best to address the problem.

1
Getting Started with the Azure IoT Platform

In this chapter, you will learn the following recipes:

- Creating Azure IoT Hub from the portal
- Creating Azure IoT Hub from the Command Prompt
- Creating Azure IoT Hub from PowerShell
- Understanding the Azure IoT Suite
- Using Azure IoT SDK
- Calculating the pricing of IoT Hub

Introduction

IoT is the next revolution in computing and is truly the first step toward a digital business. Connected sensors, devices, and intelligent operations can transform businesses and enable new growth opportunities. A critical part of IoT is cloud-based solutions that enable you to connect, secure, and manage IoT devices, as well as providing deep insights from IoT data. Microsoft Azure is an all-in-one IoT platform which provides ways to implement end-to-end IoT solutions.

The recipes in this chapter will primarily focus on getting you started with the Microsoft Azure IoT platform, understanding the IoT lifecycle, and each phase of the IoT solution, followed by which, we will also consider how to create an IoT Hub and how the IoT Hub endpoints work. You will also be introduced to the Azure IoT Suite introduction. We will go through the sizing of different IoT Hub instances and will end with pricing calculations for IoT Hubs. IoT Hub is a central connection point for IoT devices and IoT solution, the features Hub supports are IoT specific.

Getting started with the Microsoft Azure IoT platform

Microsoft Azure supports connectivity, data ingestion, storage, to analytics using a diverse set of cloud offerings. One can easily adopt the Microsoft platform for reliable and secure IoT device-to-cloud communication when you build any IoT solution.

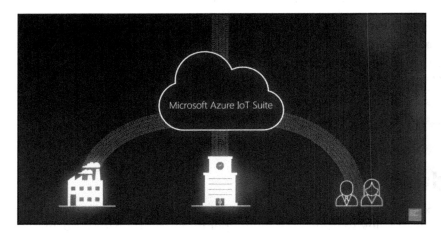

Azure IoT Suite image from Microsoft documentation

Components of the IoT platform

Today, IoT is described using various definitions; however, it essentially consists of four basic areas:

- **Things**: Any physical thing, such as line-of-business assets, including industry devices or sensors

- **Connectivity**: Those things that have connectivity to the internet
- **Data**: Those things that can collect and communicate information – this information may include data collected from the environment
- **Analytics**: The analytics that come with the data produce insight and enable people or machines to take actions that drive business outcomes

Microsoft's IoT platform's core foundation is the Azure cloud platform; it has a set of services to help companies achieve the benefits of implementing an IoT strategy. Microsoft's Azure IoT services are a set of IoT capabilities, outlined in the following, enabling enterprises to build and realize value from IoT solutions quickly and efficiently. As part of core IoT offerings, Microsoft Azure IoT services enable Microsoft to meet the customers wherever they are in their IoT journey – whether they are focused on where to start, or are ready to scale IoT scenarios which will transform their digital business.

The Azure IoT approach to providing such an IoT platform is built on three foundational pillars. These IoT services set Microsoft apart from other vendors – no other vendor delivers the breadth of capabilities, enterprise level service, and scale that Microsoft does.

- **Comprehensive technology**: The most comprehensive set of IoT technologies, to help customers connect, analyze, and act on insights
- **Enterprise focus**: The services are built on an enterprise grade cloud that take advantage of all the scalability and security features we have enabled in our cloud
- **Global scale**: By leveraging Azure IoT services, customers can seamlessly scale from **Proof of Concept** (**PoC**) to global deployment on Microsoft's hyper-scale worldwide infrastructure

Microsoft Azure IoT platform

The IoT solutions offered by Microsoft Azure are broadly divided into two categories. These are Azure IoT Suite and Azure IoT Hub. IoT solutions, including Azure IoT Suite and Azure IoT Hub, harness the power of our full cloud, data and developer offerings for the enterprise to provide hyper-scale IoT services, rich data and analytics, and deep integration. The IoT Suite is generally used by developers to build custom solutions using IoT SDKs. Microsoft Azure IoT SDK are open source are easily available to download from GitHub. It supports various language like C#, Node.JS, C, and Java. you can use any machine which is capable of development with these technologies.

The Azure IoT offerings are customizable to fit the unique needs of organizations. It will provides finished applications to speed deployment of common scenarios we see across many industries. Some example of such common scenarios are remote monitoring, asset management and predictive maintenance. It can grow and scale solutions to millions of things. The Azure platform provides a simple pricing model while providing a rich set of capabilities, so companies can plan and budget appropriately. This approach is aimed at simplifying the complexities that often exist with implementing and costing IoT solutions. Along with this, Microsoft and its partners also provide a workshop in which one can identify IoT scenarios, and at the end of this workshop, they can decide to work on common goals. These workshops have various stages starting right from business problem identification, implementing PoC, to development and trials with organizational readiness and implementing it across an organization to achieve the business outcome following the path for the digitization of the business.

Developers can start building custom solutions using IoT Hub or get started quickly with the comprehensive pre-configured solutions of Azure IoT Suite (which includes Azure IoT Hub). This book will focus mostly on Azure IoT Hub and IoT Suite.

Creating Azure IoT Hub from the portal

Microsoft Azure is a leading PaaS service provider. The Azure IoT Hub is nothing but a fully managed service that enables secure and bidirectional communication with millions of IoT enabled devices using IoT protocols such as HTTPS, AMQP, and MQTT. It helps to connect, control, and manage these devices. Microsoft Azure provides easy-to-easy IoT SDK, which are available in various languages, such as C#, C, Node.js, and so on.

Getting ready

Azure IoT Hub provides:

- Device identity and registry
- Device-to-cloud and cloud-to-device communication, including one way or bidirectional
- It also supports file transfer messages
- We can query the device store information to find out device properties, firmware versions, and other configurations
- SDK for most platforms and languages to support development

- Secure authentication on a per-device basis
- Monitoring for devices and messages

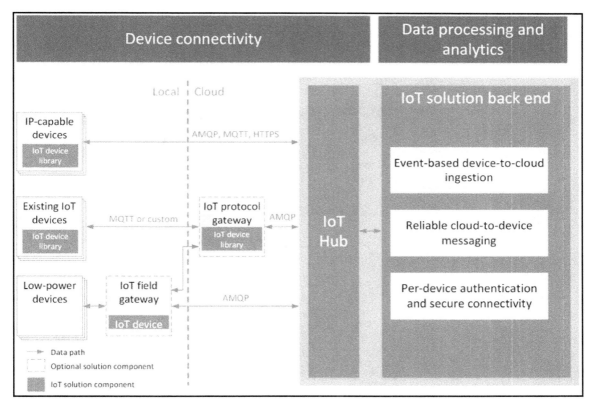

Azure IoT Hub diagram from Microsoft Azure documentation

How to do it...

To create your first IoT Hub, you will need a Microsoft Azure account. You can easily get registered on `Azure.com`.

Once you have access, you can follow the steps to create your IoT Hub:

1. Log in to `https://portal.azure.com`.
2. Once you are logged in, click on the **New** menu:

3. This blade will show all the Azure services available, we need to expand the **Internet of Things** and hit the **IoT Hub**, as shown in the following:

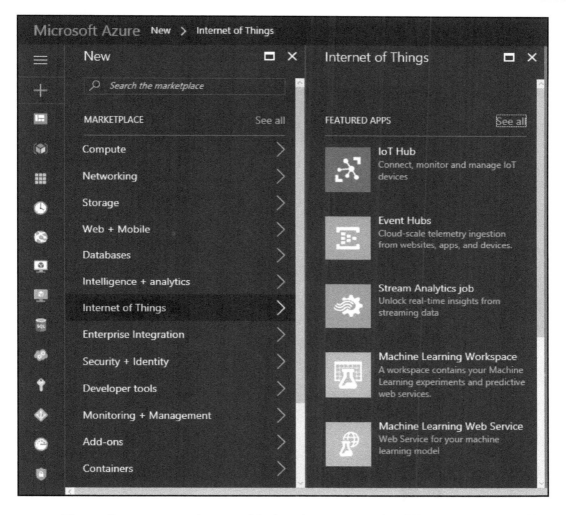

4. This will come up with a new blade, where we need to fill in the details and hit the button to the create IoT Hub:
   - We will give the **Name** as `IoTHubCookeBook`
   - **Pricing and scale tier** should be **F1 - Free**

Microsoft Azure provides free tier. This is useful for learning, as well as to evaluate any PoC on how the IoT solution will be developed.

5. We will select the data center of our choice from the list of the many available.

6. Partitions: A default value is set when the IoT Hub is created. You can change the number of partitions through this setting:

7. Hit the **Create** button and Azure will create the free tier IoT Hub for you in a moment:

Creating Azure IoT Hub from the Command Prompt

In this recipe, you will need to use the Azure account where you will create the IoT Hub, apart from this, the Azure CLI should be installed on your machine.

To install Azure CLI, follow this URL: `https://docs.microsoft.com/en-us/azure/cli-install-nodejs`.

How to do it...

In this section, let's look at creating an IoT Hub using CLI:

1. Open the Command Prompt within administrator mode.
2. Use the `login` command in Command Prompt:

```
azure login
```

3. It will ask you to login using a web browser with the link displayed in the Command Prompt:

Login command

4. The web link will validate the code generated in Command Prompt:

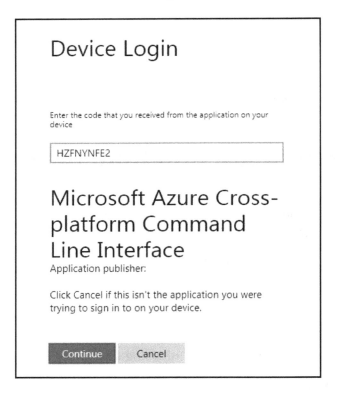

Login authenticate through web

5. Once you successfully log in, it will show a message on the browser and you can go back to the Command Prompt for your work:

Microsoft Azure Cross-platform Command Line Interface

You have signed in to the Microsoft Azure Cross-platform Command Line Interface application on your device. You may now close this window.

Login validated successfully

6. Now, select the account with which you want to work and create the IoT Hub:

```
azure account set "Visual Studio Enterprise"
```

```
C:\WINDOWS\system32>azure account set "Visual Studio Enterprise"
info:    Executing command account set
info:    Setting subscription to "Visual Studio Enterprise" with id
info:    Changes saved
info:    account set command OK

C:\WINDOWS\system32>
```

Select Azure account

7. Now, we need to create a resource group, which this IoT Hub will be a part of:

```
azure group create -n MyBookIoTHub -l westus
```

8. We use the following command to create a new IoT Hub using the Command Prompt:

```
azure iothub create -g MyBookIoTHub -n MyBookIoTHub -l westus -k s1
-u 1
```

In the preceding create IoT Hub command, the parameters are resource group, IoT Hub name, location, instance size, and unit.

Creating Azure IoT Hub from PowerShell

In this recipe, you will need to use the Azure account where you will create the IoT Hub. Apart from this Azure PowerShell should be installed on your machine.

To install PowerShell, follow this URL: `https://docs.microsoft.com/en-gb/powershell/azure/install-azurerm-ps?view=azurermps-4.2.0`.

How to do it...

Let's look at this section to create IoT Hub using PowerShell:

1. Open PowerShell in administrator mode:

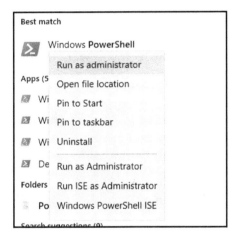

Start PowerShell in administrator mode

2. Once the PowerShell window is ready, log in to the Azure account using the command:

   `'Login-AzureRmAccount'`

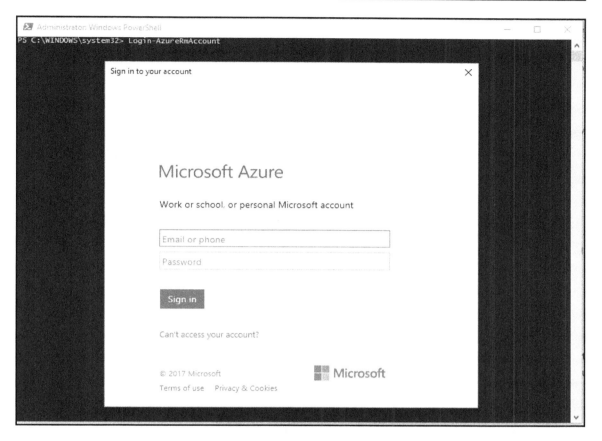

Login to Azure account

3. If you have only one Azure subscription, then you are good to go.

4. If you have multiple subscriptions, first we need to select the subscription which we need to work on.

5. To view a list of all the available Azure subscription for your work use the following command:

```
'Get-AzureRMSubscription'
```

6. Select the subscription with the command, (in my case it is Visual Studio Enterprise):

```
Select-AzureRMSubscription -SubscriptionName "{subscription name}"
```

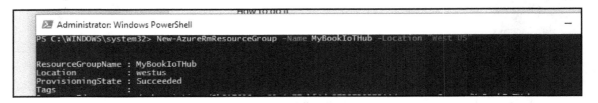

Select the Azure account to work with

7. Before we create the IoT Hub, we need to create a resource group, which this IoT Hub will be a part of.

8. The command to create a new resource group is the following:

```
New-AzureRmResourceGroup -Name MyBookIoTHub -Location "West US"
```

Add new resource group

9. We will create the IoT Hub using the following command:

```
New-AzureRmIotHub `
 -ResourceGroupName MyBookIoTHub `
 -Name MyBookIoTHub `
 -SkuName S1 -Units 1 `
 -Location "West US"
```

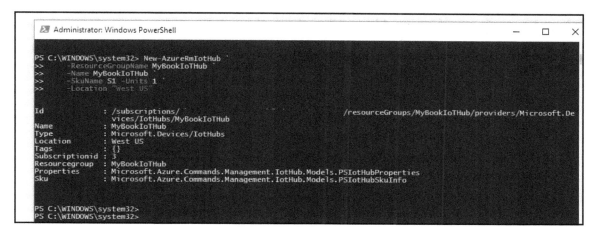

Azure IoT Hub created

10. You can log in to the Azure portal and view the newly created IoT Hub:

IoT Hub list view

11. To view the available IoT Hub in your account, use the command:

```
Get-AzureRmIotHub
```

12. To delete an existing IoT Hub, use the following command:

```
Remove-AzureRmIotHub `
 -ResourceGroupName MyBookIoTHub `
 -Name MyBookIoTHub
```

Understanding the Azure IoT Suite

The Azure IoT Suite is a set of Azure services that provides you with a complete solution which helps with the following:

- Collecting data from devices
- Analyzing data streams in-motion
- Storing and querying large datasets
- Visualizing both real-time and historical data
- Integrating with backend systems
- Managing your devices

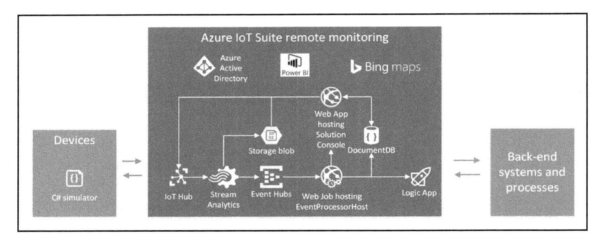

IoT Suite architecture from Microsoft Azure documentation

The Azure IoT Suite can connect with a broad range of devices with the help of IoT SDKs. The data generated by devices can be any operational data.

These devices can send that data to the Azure IoT Hub using the Azure IoT cloud gateway. The IoT solution backend receives, processes, and stores the data from these devices. The Azure IoT and Power BI enables you to analyse the data and present it in the form of dashboards or Power BI reports.

How to do it...

We will understand pre-configured solutions in this section:

- What is a pre-configured solution?
- How remote monitoring works
- How predictive maintenance works
- How connected factory works

How it works...

Microsoft helps companies to take advantage of IoT to transform business outcomes by providing pre-configured solutions under IoT Suite, a common IoT solution pattern to reduce the time for initial base development. This is comprised of multiple Azure services which are a part of the Microsoft IoT platform. The source code is also available on GitHub, using which, one can customize the solution as per specific business scenarios.

Pre-configured solutions

Azure IoT Suite provides two common IoT solution patterns. Each solution is end-to-end, built along with the simulator to generate the telemetry data. These solutions give you the starting point for your IoT case, as well as a lesson on how a common IoT scenario works.

Microsoft Azure IoT provides three common scenarios in the form of pre-configured solutions with IoT Suite:

Remote monitoring: This preconfigured solution connects and monitors devices. Once we deploy the remote monitoring suite on Azure subscription, it also provides a simulator and these simulated devices will keep on generating data for these devices. Once the data is ingested, it will be processed against a set of rules and the data will then be presented on the dashboard. It uses a Bing map to show the live location of the devices.

Predictive maintenance: Predictive maintenance is another common IoT scenario. This solution, once deployed, starts automatically simulating the data. It also provides a predictive model, which is helpful in the case of asset maintenance. In `Chapter 6`, *IoT Suite and Pre-Configured Solutions,* we will be creating pre-configured solutions.

Connected factory: When you deploy the connected factory pre-configured solution, this solution is built with a common industrial scenario. In this scenario, factories can be connected to the solution, thus reporting the data values required to find out **overall equipment efficiency** (**OEE**) and **key performance indicators** (**KPIs**) for the factory operations. The following sections show you how to:

- Monitor factory, production lines, station OEE, and KPI values
- Analyze the telemetry data generated from these devices using Azure Time Series Insights
- Act on alerts to fix issues

It also provides the dashboard view for these actions and operations as a part of this solution.

Using Azure IoT SDK

Azure provides SDK for the device side as well as the PaaS services which are a part of its IoT stack. Microsoft Azure IoT SDK are open source are easily available to download from GitHub. It supports various language like C#, Node.JS, C, Java. you can use any machine which is capable of development with these technologies.

Azure IoT device SDK, which runs on the IoT device side enables the device for communicating with the IoT Hub. It uses the protocols available. The application deployed on the device then sends the telemetry data to cloud. For this purpose, the device needs to be registered with the IoT Hub as well. These SDKs also help run the bidirectional commands which make it easy to control and manage the device.

Getting ready

Currently these IoT device SDKs support different programming languages, such as ANSI C using .NET C#, and for Java, Node.js and Python as well.

Likewise, these SDKs also support various OS and platforms on which we can develop the applications. Microsoft has made these SDKs portable on any platform and OS. By making these SDKs open source, they are readily available for download on GitHub to make any customization as per your needs.

How to do it...

Azure IoT service SDK provides the code that is used in building an IoT application that directly works with the IoT Hub. It will enable you to manage devices, read messages sent by devices, or even send commands to devices to control actions at the device end.

The GitHub URL to download these open source SDK's are:

- `Azure IoT service SDK for .NET`
- `Azure IoT service SDK for Node.js`
- `Azure IoT service SDK for Java`
- `Azure IoT service SDK for Python`

Azure IoT gateway SDKs are used to simplify the connectivity to IoT Hub when we have scenarios which vary drastically between industries, and even between customers within the same industry. The Azure IoT gateway SDK can be used to implement custom-made IoT solutions for your scenario. The device SDKs can be used to implement an IoT client that facilitates connectivity to the cloud. It simply uses the supported communication protocol, it will extract and process the data using the protocol supported before sending it to the cloud.

See also

Download the source code for IoT gateway SDK from GitHub: `https://github.com/Azure/azure-iot-gateway-sdk`.

Calculating the pricing of IoT Hub

IoT Hub is offered in four editions: Free, S1, S2, and S3. IoT Hub is generally available. In this section, we will understand the different instance sizes and will apply a calculation to find the pricing of IoT Hub. This will help you to identify the right size, and right cost for your IoT solution.

Getting ready

The pricing table based on Microsoft Azure IoT Hub pricing is as follows:

Instance	Price	Message/Day	Message size
Free	$ 0	8,000	0.5 KB
S1	$ 50	400,000	4 KB
S2	$ 500	6,000,000	4 KB
S3	$ 5,000	300,000,000	4 KB

How to do it...

To find out the what will be the price based on the IoT solution needs we will use the pricing calculator provided by Microsoft Azure:

1. The price is per size of the IoT Hub instance.
2. First find out the size and units per size required.
3. First use the following link to go to Azure pricing calculator:

   ```
   https://azure.microsoft.com/en-gb/pricing/calculator/
   ```

4. Now select the Azure service for which you want to estimate the price, in our case it is **IoT Hub**:

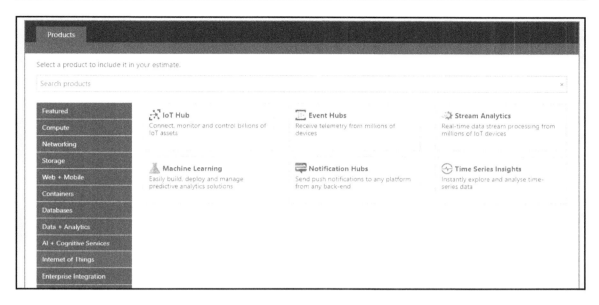

Select the service for estimation

5. Once you have selected IoT Hub service, it will show the estimation area:

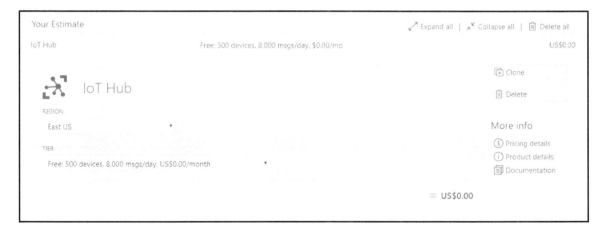

IoT Hub selected for price estimation

6. Select the IoT Hub tier based on the number of messages per day capability you want to build in your IoT solution:

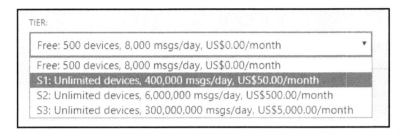

Select the IoT Hub tier

7. Select the number of units required to full fill your requirement amount of messages per day:

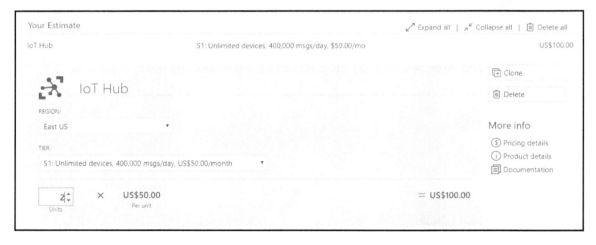

Set the units for selected tier

8. I have selected S1 tier with 2 units. It will support 800 k messages per day at $100.

There's more...

Let's consider an example to understand how the pricing works.

A device ingests the 1 KB device-to-cloud message size data per minute to the IoT Hub. The solution backend invokes a method (with 512 bytes of payload) on the device every ten minutes to trigger a specific action. The device responds to the method with a result of 200 bytes.

The device consumes 1 message * 60 minutes * 24 hours = 1440 messages per day for the device-to-cloud messages, and 2 requests plus responses * 6 times per hour * 24 hours = 288 messages for the methods, for a total of 1728 messages per day.

See also

You can refer to Microsoft documentation for similar examples; click here `https://docs.mi` `crosoft.com/en-us/azure/iot-hub/iot-hub-devguide-pricing`.

2
Introducing Device Management

In this chapter, you will learn the following recipes:

- Device registry operations
- Device twins
- Device direct methods
- Device jobs
- IoT Hub query explorer

Introduction

Azure IoT Hub has capabilities that can be used by a developer to build robust device management. There could be different use cases or scenarios across multiple industries, but these device management capabilities, their patterns, and the SDK code remains the same, saving significant time in developing and managing, along with maintaining millions of devices.

Device management will be the central part of any IoT solution. The IoT solution helps users to manage devices remotely, take actions from cloud-based applications such as disable, update data, run any command, and firmware updates.

In this chapter, we are going to perform all these tasks for device management, and we will start with creating the device.

Understanding IoT Hub endpoints

IoT Hub provides built-in endpoints that can be easily used with IoT SDK. The following image with reference from the Microsoft Azure IoT documentation gives a snapshot of all the endpoints an IoT Hub gives:

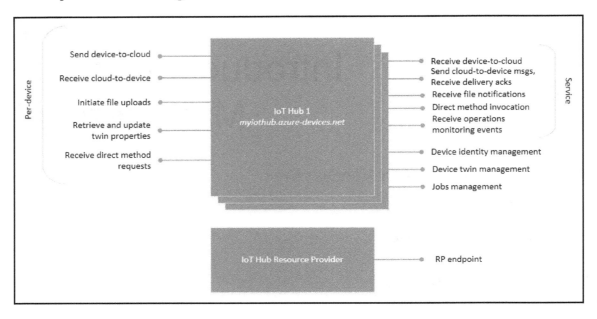

IoT Hub endpoints, reference from Azure IoT documentation

IoT Hub provides HTTP rest APIs for device provisioning. These device identities are used for authentication purposes with access controls. This endpoint provides different operations to manage devices:

- **Create devices**: Using the create method, you can easily create a device in the IoT Hub. This will create and assign a unique key to each device, which will be required for each communication of that device.
- **Update devices**: Using update device API, we are able to control the current state of the device, whether to disable or enable the device.

- **Delete devices by using deviceId**: If device is no longer required to be registered or communicated with, we can remove it from the Hub using the delete API.
- **Some of the other useful operations are**:
    - Retrieve devices by using `deviceId`
    - List up to 1000 device identities
    - Import device identities from Azure Blob storage
    - Export all device identities to Azure Blob storage

The export all device identities operation is the way in which you can export all the devices in IoT Hub in one go into a file, which will be stored on the Blob storage.

For each IoT enabled device that is provisioned and registered with IoT Hub, it provides device endpoints which expose the sent or received message endpoints.

A message from device-to-cloud is sent through a device-facing endpoint, then internally, IoT Hub puts these messages for the devices. You can pull these messages using device registration details such as the device ID and device key. In the coming chapters, we will be doing this practically.

Other frequently used endpoints are cloud-to-device, which act as the route for bidirectional communication.

IoT Hub has started supporting file ingestion also. When we have a large file to upload or a batch of telemetry, file ingestion is best suited for these scenarios.

We can configure the blob storage account within IoT Hub and, using the device IoT SDKs, the file will be uploaded. On completion, IoT Hub will check and publish a message for service endpoints to work further on the data.

Device twin is a document store collection of all devices, in which each collection can store multiple device's metadata, configurations and so on. A device twin is useful for storing a device's specific details in the cloud, finding out the current state of the device. Whenever a device or backend system needs to sync device information, a device twin is used which holds the latest state of it.

Direct methods is a way IoT Hub helps to control a device directly such as an HTTP communication. When we want a result or an action to be taken by a device, a direct method is used, where we immediately get a response from the device through this communication.

A service endpoint enables any backend system to interact with the IoT Hub. These endpoints allow the backend to perform operations such as:

- Receiving cloud-to-device messages.
- Sending cloud-to-device messages and getting an acknowledgement for the same.
- File ingestion officiation, if this method is used for telemetry.
- Direct method invocation. A backend system can invoke any direct method on the device.

Scheduling jobs on multiple devices is a way in which we can perform an operation in bulk. For example, if we need to update device properties for a set of devices or invoke some direct methods on a group of devices, this is useful at the execution level.

A backend application can schedule the activities planned for a group of devices.

Device registry operations

This sample application is focused on device registry operations and how they work. We will create a console application as our first IoT solution and look at the various device management techniques.

Getting ready

Let's create a console application to start with IoT:

1. Create a new project in Visual Studio:

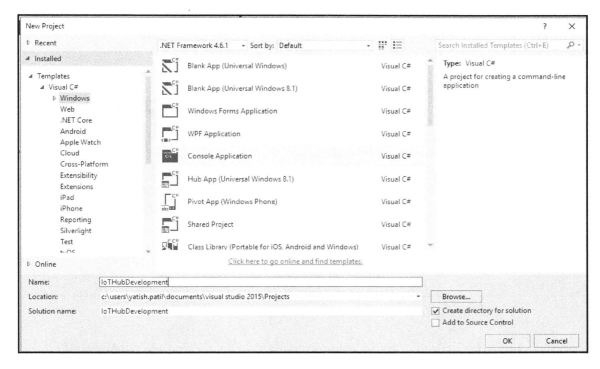

Create a console application

2. Add the IoT Hub connectivity extension in Visual Studio:

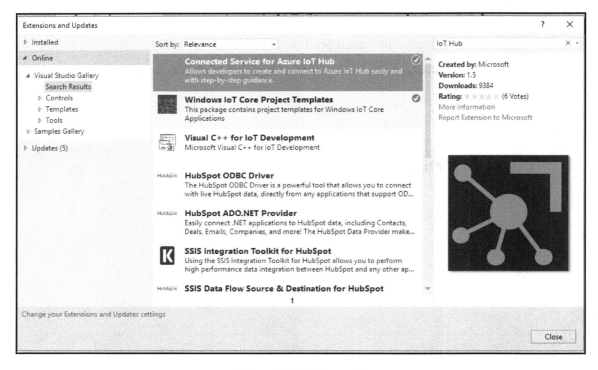

Add the extension for IoT Hub connectivity

3. Now, right-click on the **Solution** in Visual Studio, navigate to **Add,** and select **Connected Services.**

4. Select Azure IoT Hub and click on **Add.**

5. Now, select the Azure subscription from the dropdown, followed by which you will get a list of the IoT Hub service parts of this Azure account, which you can select:

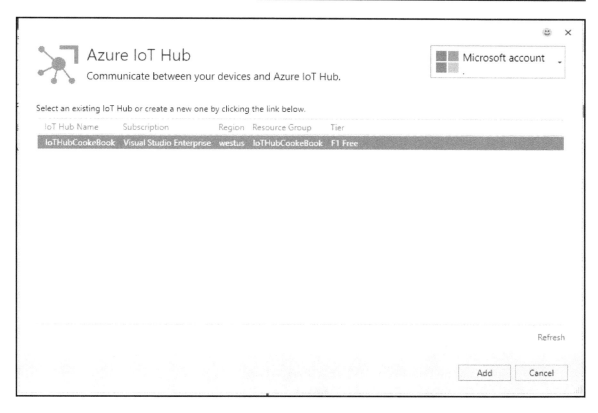

Select IoT Hub for our application

6. Next, it will ask you to add a device; or you can skip this step, and click on the **Add** button, which will add the connected service to the **Solution**.

How to do it...

In this section, we will start with registering the new device, followed by some more device management operations such as: retrieve, delete, list, export, and import.

1. Create a device identity by initializing the Azure IoT Hub registry connection:

```
string deviceId = "myFirstDevice";
registryManager =
RegistryManager.CreateFromConnectionString(connectionString);
Device device = new Device();
        try
```

```
        {
                device = await registryManager.AddDeviceAsync(new
Device(deviceId));
                success = true;
        }
                catch (DeviceAlreadyExistsException)
                {
                        success = false;
        }
}
```

2. Retrieve the device identity by `deviceId`:

```
string deviceId = "myFirstDevice";
Device device = new Device();
 try
 {
 device = await registryManager.GetDeviceAsync(deviceId);
 }
 catch (DeviceAlreadyExistsException)
 {
 return device;
 }
```

3. Delete the device identity:

```
string deviceId = "myFirstDevice";
Device device = new Device();
 try
 {
    device = GetDevice(deviceId);
    await registryManager.RemoveDeviceAsync(device);
    success = true;
 }
 catch (Exception ex)
 {
 success = false;
 }
```

4. Disable the IoT device from the device registry. This can be handled through an IoT solution in certain scenarios, such as if the device is tampered with or these are some critical issues with the device:

```
string deviceId = "myFirstDevice";
Device device = new Device();
  try
  {
    device = GetDevice(deviceId);
```

```
   device.Status = DeviceStatus.Disabled;
   // Update the device registry
   await registryManager.UpdateDeviceAsync(device);
   success = true;
}
catch (Exception ex)
{
    success = false;
  }
```

5. List up to 1000 identities:

```
try
  {
  var devicelist = registryManager.GetDevicesAsync(1000);
  return devicelist.Result;
  }
  catch (Exception ex)
  {
  //
```

6. Export all the identities to Azure Blob storage:

```
var blobClient = storageAccount.CreateCloudBlobClient();

string Containername = "iothubdevices";

//Get a reference to a container
var container = blobClient.GetContainerReference(Containername);
container.CreateIfNotExists();

//Generate a SAS token
var storageUri = GetContainerSasUri(container);
await registryManager.ExportDevicesAsync(storageUri,
"devices1.txt", false);
}
```

7. Import all the identities to Azure Blob storage:

```
await registryManager.ImportDevicesAsync(storageUri,
OutputStorageUri);
```

The output of `ImportDevice` methods creates a job which can be used to perform bulk operation like `create` and `delete`.

How it works...

Let's now understand the steps we performed. We initiated this by creating a console application and configured it for the Azure IoT Hub solution. The idea behind this was look at a simple operation for device management.

In this section, we started with a simple operation for the provision of the device by adding it to the IoT Hub. We needed to create a connection to the IoT Hub first. The next step will creating the object of the registry manager. This registry manager object is used to perform the device identity operations.

Once we are connected with IoT Hub using the SDK, we can perform operations such as adding a device, deleting a device, and getting a device; these methods are asynchronous ones.

IoT Hub also connects with Azure Blob storage for bulk operations, such as exporting all devices or importing all devices; this works on JSON format only. The entire set of IoT devices gets exported in this way.

There's more...

Device identities are represented as JSON documents. They consists of properties such as:

- `deviceId`: This represents the unique identification or the IoT device
- `ETag`: This is a string representing a weak `ETag` for the device identity
- `symkey`: This is a composite object containing a primary and a secondary key, stored in base64 format
- `status`: If enabled, the device can connect with IoT Hub. If disabled, this device cannot access any device-facing endpoint
- `statusReason`: A string that can be used to store the reason for status changes
- `connectionState`: It can be connected or disconnected

Device twins

Firstly, we need to understand what a device twin is. We will be following some steps to use a device twin to understand their purpose and where we can use the device twin in any IoT solution. The device twin is a JSON formatted document that describes the metadata, properties of any device created within IoT Hub. It describes the individual device specific information.

The device twin is made up of: tags, desired properties, and reported properties. The operations that can be done on an IoT device is to update the data or query for any IoT device. this feature can be built into the IoT Solution from where a Administrator user can initiate these.

Tags hold the device metadata that can be accessed from an IoT solution only. The desired properties are set from the IoT solution and can be accessed on the device. Whereas the reported properties are set on the device and retrieved at the IoT solution end.

As per Microsoft Azure, currently, the MQTT protocol is the only protocol supported for working with the device twin.

How to do it...

Let's follow the following steps to use the device twin operation:

1. Store the device metadata:

```
var patch = new
{
properties = new
{
desired = new
{
deviceConfig = new
{
configId = Guid.NewGuid().ToString(),
DeviceOwner = "yatish",
latitude = "17.5122560",
longitude = "70.7760470"

}
},
reported = new
{
deviceConfig = new
{
configId = Guid.NewGuid().ToString(),
DeviceOwner = "yatish",
latitude = "17.5122560",
longitude = "70.7760470"

}
}
},
```

```
tags = new
{
location = new
{
region = "US",
plant = "Redmond43"
}
}

};

 await registryManager.UpdateTwinAsync(deviceTwin.DeviceId,
JsonConvert.SerializeObject(patch), deviceTwin.ETag);
```

2. Query the device metadata:

```
var query = registryManager.CreateQuery("SELECT * FROM devices
WHERE deviceId = '" + deviceTwin.DeviceId + "'");
```

3. Report the current state of the device:

```
var results = await query.GetNextAsTwinAsync();
```

How it works...

In this sample, we retrieved the current information of the device twin and updated the desired properties, which were accessible on the device side. In the code, we set the coordinates of the device with latitude and longitude values, the device owner name, and so on. This same value will be accessible on the device side.

In a similar manner, we can set some properties on the device side which will be a part of the reported properties. While using the device twin, we must always consider:

- Tags can be set, read, and accessed only by the backend
- The reported properties are set by a device and can be read by the backend
- The desired properties are set by the backend and can be read by the backend
- We can use the read-only version and the last updated properties elements to detect updates when necessary

 Each device twin size is limited to 8 KB per device in the IoT Hub.

There's more...

Device twin metadata always maintains the last updated timestamp for any modifications. This is the UTC timestamp maintained in the metadata.

Device twin format is a JSON format in which the `tags`, `desired`, and `reported` properties are stored; here is a sample JSON with different nodes showing how it is stored:

```
"tags": {
  "$etag": "1234321",
   "location": {
    "country": "India"
    "city": "Mumbai",
    "zipCode": "400001"
  }
},
"properties": {
  "desired": {
    "latitude": 18.75,
    "longitude": -75.75,
    "status": 1,
    "$version": 4
  },
  "reported": {
    "latitude": 18.75,
    "longitude": -75.75,
    "status": 1,
    "$version": 4
  }
}
```

Device direct methods

Azure IoT Hub provides fully managed bidirectional communication between the IoT solution on the backend and the IoT devices in the fields. We will be considering detailed message communication in `Chapter 3`, *IoT Hub Messaging and Commands*.

When there is a need for an immediate communication result, a direct method best suits these scenarios. Let's take an example of a home automation system. One needs to control the AC temperature or turn the faucet showers on/off. It uses the HTTP protocol for method invocation.

How to do it...

The following steps will be taken to perform a direct method with an IoT device connected with IoT Hub:

1. Invoke this method from the application:

```
public async Task<CloudToDeviceMethodResult>
InvokeDirectMethodOnDevice(string deviceId, ServiceClient
serviceClient)
 {
 var methodInvocation = new CloudToDeviceMethod("WriteToMessage") {
ResponseTimeout = TimeSpan.FromSeconds(300) };
 methodInvocation.SetPayloadJson("'1234567890'");

 var response = await
serviceClient.InvokeDeviceMethodAsync(deviceId, methodInvocation);

 return response;
 }
```

2. Direct method execution on the IoT device:

```
deviceClient = DeviceClient.CreateFromConnectionString("",
TransportType.Mqtt);

 deviceClient.SetMethodHandlerAsync("WriteToMessage", new
DeviceSimulator().WriteToMessage, null).Wait();

 deviceClient.SetMethodHandlerAsync("GetDeviceName", new
DeviceSimulator().GetDeviceName, new
DeviceData("DeviceClientMethodMqttSample")).Wait();
```

How it works...

The direct method works on a request-response interaction with the IoT device and backend solutions. The direct method has a timeout. If no reply is received within that expected time, the direct method will fail. These synchronous requests have, by default, 30 seconds of timeout; one can modify the timeout and increase it up to 3600 seconds, depending on the IoT scenarios you have. The device needs to connect using the MQTT protocol, whereas the backend solution can use HTTP.

The JSON data size for direct method can work up to 8 KB.

Device jobs

In a typical scenario, the device administrator or operators are required to manage devices in bulk. In the earlier sections, we looked at the device twin, which maintains properties and tags. Conceptually, the job is nothing but a wrapper on the possible actions, which can be done in bulk.

Suppose we have a scenario in which we need to update the properties for multiple devices; in such a case, one can schedule the job and track the progress of the job. I would like to set the frequency to send the data every 1 hour instead of every 30 minutes for 1000 IoT devices. Another example could be to reboot multiple devices at the same time.

 Device administrators can perform device registrations in bulk using the export and import methods.

How to do it...

In this section, we will create a device job to update the device twin properties:

1. We will create a job to update device twin properties:

```
var twin = new Twin();
twin.Properties.Desired["HighTemperature"] = "44";
twin.Properties.Desired["City"] = "Mumbai";
twin.ETag = "*";

return await jobClient.ScheduleTwinUpdateAsync(jobId,
"deviceId='"+ deviceId + "'",
twin,
DateTime.Now,
10);
```

2. We will use following code to get the device job status, which was initiated in step 1:

```
JobClient jobClient;
JobClient jobClient;jobClient =
JobClient.CreateFromConnectionString(abc.GetConnectionString());

public  async Task<JobResponse> MonitorJob(string jobId, JobClient
jobClient)
{
return  await jobClient.GetJobAsync(jobId);
}
```

How it works...

In this example, we looked at a job updating the device twin information, and we can follow up the job for its status to find out whether the job was completed or failed. In this case, instead of having single API calls, a job can be created to execute on multiple IoT devices. The job client object provides the jobs available with the IoT Hub using the connection to it. Once we locate the job using its unique ID, we can retrieve the status for it.

The code snippet mentioned in the *How to do it...* section uses the temperature properties and updates the data. The job is scheduled to start execution immediately with a 10-second execution timeout set.

There's more...

For a job, the life cycle begins with the initiation from the IoT solution. If any job is in execution, we can query to it and see the status of the execution.

Another common scenario where this could be useful is the firmware update, reboot, configuration updates; apart from the device property read or write.

Each device job has properties that helps us to work with them. The useful properties are start and end date time, status, and lastly, device job statistics, which gives job execution statistics.

IoT Hub query explorer

IoT Hub supports a SQL-like language to retrieve information regarding device twins, jobs, and message routing. Basically, you can write a basic SQL command and that will be executed against the device registry.

Each query follows the syntax like SQL; it has the standard SELECT, FROM, and WHERE keywords used to retrieve the result set in the result window.

How to do it...

In this section, we will follow the steps to use the query explorer and retrieve the device information in the results window:

1. we will select the IoT Hub IoTHubCookBook service from the Azure portal.
2. Select **Query Explorer**:

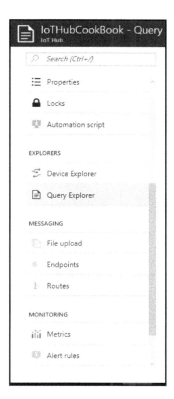

3. Using the execution windows, type the query you want to execute:

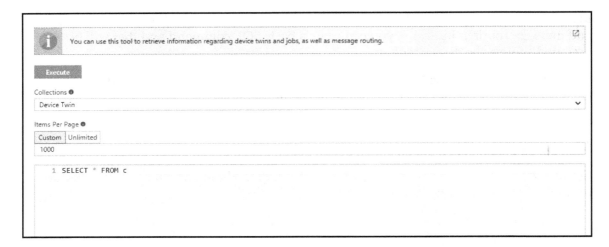

4. The output will be shown in the result window:

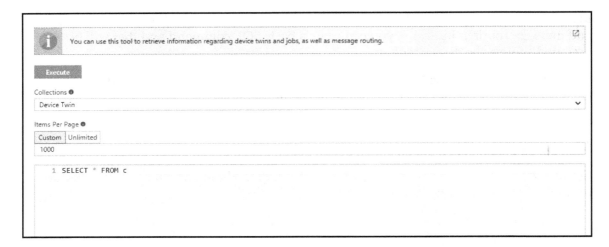

There's more...

IoT Hub query explorer is easy to use on the collection of the device registry. Some of the sample queries will be as follows:

```
SELECT * FROM devices
```

We tried a simple query which selects all devices. Now, let's try to query using the device tags and device twin. we will refer to the desired properties field called as `DeviceOwner`.

```
SELECT * FROM devices
WHERE tags.location.region = 'US'
AND properties.desired.deviceConfig.DeviceOwner = 'Rudra'
```

3
IoT Hub Messaging and Commands

In this chapter, you will learn the following recipes:

- Messaging - device-to-cloud
- Processing device-to-cloud messaging
- Messaging - commands and control
- File uploads with IoT Hub
- Device firmware updates

Introduction

IoT Hub provides messaging, which is reliable and durable, by providing the following two types of communication between devices and IoT backend solutions:

- Send device-to-cloud messages
- Send cloud-to-device messages

IoT Hub implements at least once delivery guarantees for the messages. That means, when using device-to-cloud and cloud-to-device messaging, it will deliver the messages at least once. IoT Hub currently supports different devices: facing protocols mostly known as MQTT, AMQP, and HTTPS.

IoT Hub has defined a common message format, so that all device-facing protocols the communication work seamlessly. To make sure our devices are running as we expect them to, we will also want to be notified of our IoT device's state, which can be either be running or stopped. IoT Hub is built on technologies like event hubs and service bus to facilitate this device-to-cloud or cloud-to-device messaging containing the device data or response to any command.

IoT Hub provides bidirectional, asymmetrical ways of communicating between the device and the cloud.

Messaging - device-to-cloud

The IoT Hub device-to-cloud messaging, which is referred to as telemetry data, is implemented as a streaming messaging pattern. The telemetry can be sensor data collected by the IoT device, along with the timestamp and metadata for the device. IoT Hub exposes the endpoints that will enable the device-to-cloud messages. The default route is `/devices//messages/events`, which is compatible with event hubs. Once the IoT Hub is configured for message routing, the routing rules engine then routes your messages to one of the service-facing endpoints on your IoT Hub which are sent from the IoT devices, example a temperature sensor is sending data, suppose the temperature falls below 25 C it will be routed to custom endpoints.

IoT Hub also provides the message routing mechanism while sending the device-to-cloud message. When we have many IoT devices out in the field sending the data, there could be scenarios where an immediate action is required, such as an alarm which indicates a serious problem. Some of these can be detected for anomalies. example could be a device connected to your home door sending alert if any theft alerts detected by IoT device.

While other messages can be just for storage purposes. Some analytics can be designed based on this transactional data.

Message routing is a new service built into the IoT Hub that makes it easy to deal with these scenarios and act on the alarming situation for operators. We can simply configure the routing logic in the IoT Hub, and it will take care of the rest by filtering messages and adding them to the respective queues. Lets create a new custom route:

IoT Hub message route

Next, we will be creating a device simulator and sending some telemetry data from the device.

How to do it...

We will create a simulated device:

1. Create a console application in Visual Studio and name it `SimulatedDevice`.
2. Add the `Azure.Devices.Client` package from NuGet.

3. To add any package from NuGet, you can right-click on **Solution** in Visual Studio and select **Manage NuGet Packages**.

4. Create a device connection using the following code:

```
deviceClient =
DeviceClient.CreateFromConnectionString("HostName=IoTHubCookBook.az
ure-devices.net;DeviceId=myFirstDevice;SharedAccessKey=",
TransportType.Mqtt);
```

5. Create telemetry data to be sent from this device:

```
var telemetryDataPoint = new
{
 deviceId = "minwinpc",
 windSpeed = currentWindSpeed,
 highTemp = 72.3,
 lowtemp = 11.2,
 latitude = "17.5122560",
 longitude = "70.7760470"
};
```

6. Convert this data into JSON format:

```
var messageString =
JsonConvert.SerializeObject(telemetryDataPoint);
var message = new Message(Encoding.ASCII.GetBytes(messageString));
```

7. Finally, send this device data to the cloud using the following code:

```
await deviceClient.SendEventAsync(message);
```

How it works...

In this topic, we first created a C# based console simulator, which will be act as an IoT device and sending a message to the cloud. The ingested telemetry data from the simulated IoT device is a JSON data sample being sent to the IoT Hub.

The IoT device simulator is created using a connection string; we can get this from the Azure portal, or we can form this string using the get device method we looked at in Chapter 2, *Introducing Device Management*.

Once the device has established the connection successfully, we assume it is measuring some wind speed and temperature values. In this sample application, I have considered some dummy data for the purpose of our understanding.

Similarly, you can make use of message routing feature of IoT Hub.

There's more...

The IoT Hub message format is made up of three components:

- **System properties**: This consists of message ID, expiry time, ACK feedback, and similar important system properties
- **Application properties**: This is a dictionary of string properties that the application can define and access as per the scenarios designed at the time of defining the IoT messages
- **A Binary body of device message:** This is a format which will not be easily readable as it will be in binary format making the content secure.

IoT Hub measures message size considering only the actual payload. The size in bytes is calculated as the sum of the following:

- The body size in bytes
- The size in bytes of all the values of the message system properties
- The size in bytes of all user property names and values

IoT Hub allows devices to use MQTT, MQTT over WebSockets, AMQP, AMQP over WebSockets, and HTTP protocols for device-side communications.

See also

The protocols support various portal numbers while communicating with the IoT Hub in Azure; we can find the list on the Microsoft Azure documentation for the protocols and their respective port numbers.

Processing device-to-cloud messaging

Cloud-to-device messages are important for any IoT device, which are mainly focused on some feedback or maintenance of these IoT devices. We send cloud-to-device messages through a service-facing endpoint (`/messages/devicebound`). A device receives them through a device-specific endpoint (`/devices/{deviceId}/messages/devicebound`) and takes the appropriate action on the device side based on the logic developed for the device.

These communications make the device bidirectional; some examples of bi-directional commands could be to change the configuration for a device, these fields can be time interval the device sends the data, updating some local model, size information.

How to do it...

We will be creating a simulated IoT device to send telemetry data and read that in the cloud application:

1. Create a console application in the Visual Studio simulated device.
2. Add the `Azure.Devices` package from NuGet.
3. Create an event hub client connection using the following code:

```
eventHubClient =
EventHubClient.CreateFromConnectionString(AzureIoTHub.GetConnection
String(), iotHubD2cEndpoint);
```

4. Scan through all partitions of the event hub:

```
var d2cPartitions =
eventHubClient.GetRuntimeInformation().PartitionIds;
String data = "";
foreach (string partition in d2cPartitions)
{
 var result = ReceiveMessagesFromDeviceAsync(partition);

 data = result.Result.ToString();
 if (data != "")
 return data;
}

return data;
```

5. lets use following code for reading the messages sent by the device:

```
var eventHubReceiver =
eventHubClient.GetDefaultConsumerGroup().CreateReceiver(partition,
DateTime.Now);
while (true)
{
 EventData eventData = await eventHubReceiver.ReceiveAsync();
 if (eventData == null) continue;
 var data = Encoding.UTF8.GetString(eventData.GetBytes());
 return data;
}
```

How it works...

The IoT backend application uses the SDK to process the telemetry data ingested into the IoT Hub. Depending on the message routing configuration done in the IoT Hub, the device will send those messages and they will get processed. In the preceding *How to do it...* section, we simply read the simple messages ingested by the device; and once the message is read, we can process it.

By connecting the event hub object, we can establish the connection. The event hub works on a partition basis. So here, we scan for the partition the message could be in. Once we find the message, we send it across for further processing. It could be a data transformation followed by storage in the database.

The stored data is later used by another service for analytics purposes. If any message routing is configured for alerts and actions, these can be taken immediately; and alerts can be sent to corresponding users as well through an email or text.

There's more...

IoT Hub persists all the cloud-to-device messages in the per-device queues with a default time. This makes the IoT Hub guarantee at least once device message delivery.

Each message has an `ExpiryTimeUtc` property, this `ExpiryTime` fields tells the time till the message will be persisted. We can set this `ExpiryTime` field as per our IoT solution need; We can define at the time we design the application. IoT Hub sets the state of a message to dead-lettered after its expiration time. Also, it can automatically go into the dead-lettered queue after a maximum number of retries to read the message. These properties are configurable.

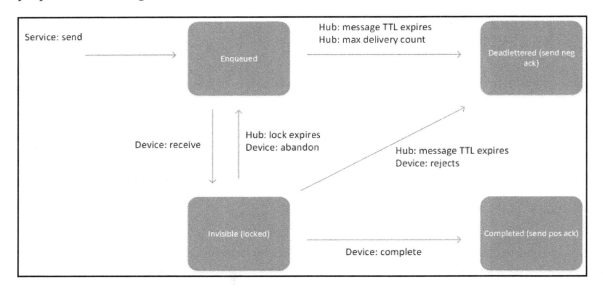

Reference from Microsoft documentation, a message lifecycle

Messaging - commands and control

Any IoT device which is capable of receiving messages from the cloud makes a bidirectional command execution easy. The device can receive the message and process upon the instruction on the hardware side. Once the action is taken, an acknowledgement is sent to the cloud about the action completion. With the IoT Hub SDK for the device and the backend application, we can achieve this. We must follow the following steps:

How to do it...

In this section we will send a cloud-to-device message. Upon receiving it, the IoT device will perform an action:

1. Send a cloud-to-device message from a cloud solution to an IoT device:

```
ServiceClient serviceClient;
serviceClient =
ServiceClient.CreateFromConnectionString(abc.GetConnectionString())
;

abc.SendCloudToDeviceMessageAsync(deviceId, serviceClient);
```

2. Prepare and send messages:

```
var commandMessage = new
Message(Encoding.ASCII.GetBytes("Close=100"));
 await serviceClient.SendAsync(deviceId, commandMessage);
```

3. The IoT device will reply by sending an acknowledgement message:

```
while (true)
{
Message receivedMessage = await deviceClient.ReceiveAsync();
if (receivedMessage == null) continue;

var cmdMessage =
Encoding.ASCII.GetString(receivedMessage.GetBytes());

// take acttion based on cmdMessage value
// ..... Some code here .....

//Send Ack to IoT Hub
await deviceClient.CompleteAsync(receivedMessage);
}
```

4. The IoT solution will process the feedback acknowledgement:

```
var feedbackReceiver = serviceClient.GetFeedbackReceiver();

while (true)
{
 var feedbackBatch = await feedbackReceiver.ReceiveAsync();
 if (feedbackBatch == null) continue;

 // take action & Udate database for action taken
```

```
foreach (var feedback in feedbackBatch.Records)
{
if (feedback.StatusCode != FeedbackStatusCode.Success)
{
// Handle compensation here
}
}

await feedbackReceiver.CompleteAsync(feedbackBatch);
}
```

How it works...

We created a service client object that will be used to send a command instruction to an IoT device. Upon receiving the command, the IoT device should take appropriate action and respond with feedback of acknowledgment to the IoT Hub.

On the cloud IoT application side, we can update the status with the command being completed by the device, which can be notified to the user/operator who is working on this device.

File uploads with IoT Hub

In most communication from IoT devices, it will send a relatively small message to IoT Hub, (up to 4 KB max allowed message size), such as telemetry data, readings, and so on. However, sometimes, we might have the need to send larger files, such as images, log files, or batch telemetry data in some scenarios.

IoT Hub provides a file ingestion method, which helps to solve this problem. Instead of sending messages through IoT Hub itself, IoT Hub instead acts as a dispatcher to an associated Azure storage configured account in IoT Hub. It uploads the files to the storage account, and then sends a notification message informing that the file ingestion has been completed. The following image is from the Microsoft Azure IoT documentation that shows how file ingestion works:

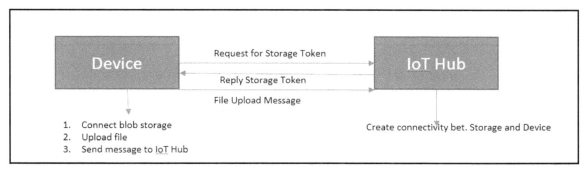

File ingestion

Devices can initiate file uploads by sending a notification through a device-facing endpoint (/devices/{deviceId}/files). When a device notifies IoT Hub of an upload having been completed, IoT Hub generates file upload notifications that can be received through a service-facing endpoint (/messages/servicebound/filenotifications) as messages, and then they are further processed as per backend application logic.

Getting ready

We need to first configure the IoT Hub for file ingestion; Blob storage needs to be configured, along with a container where the file should be uploaded.

How to do it...

We will create a device simulator to upload one sample batch telemetry data file, but before this, we need to first configure the IoT Hub. So, let's start with the steps as follows:

1. To configure IoT Hub, we need to log into the Azure portal.
2. Select IoT Hub service and navigate to the message section.
3. Select the **File upload** option; it will open a new blade in the Azure portal.

4. Select the storage account and the container for your file ingestion:

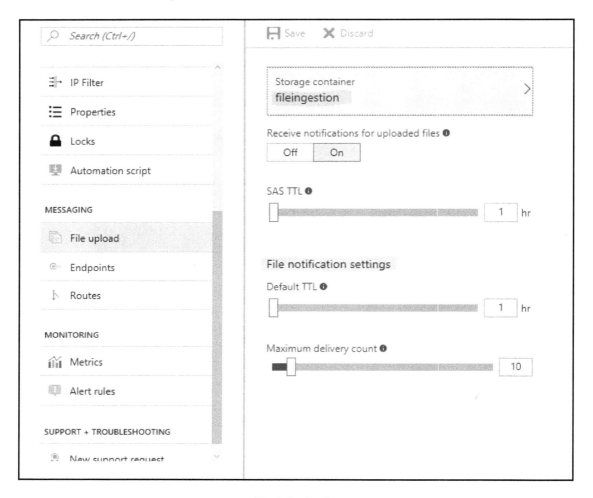

File upload configuration

5. Now, let's initiate the file upload from a device simulator:

```
using (var telemetryData = new FileStream(telemetryDataFile,
FileMode.Open))
{
 await deviceClient.UploadToBlobAsync(telemetryDataFile,
telemetryData);
}
```

6. The IoT Hub will receive the file upload notification and we will process that using the following code:

```
var notificationReceiver =
serviceClient.GetFileNotificationReceiver();
while (true)
{
 var fileUploadNotification = await
notificationReceiver.ReceiveAsync();
 if (fileUploadNotification == null) continue;

 var downoadFile = fileUploadNotification.BlobName;
 // Download the File uploaded on Blob storage
 // process the File data
 // ......
 // ......

 await notificationReceiver.CompleteAsync(fileUploadNotification);
}
```

How it works...

File ingestion works with very simple steps; the Azure storage account is configured through the Azure portal by selecting the file upload option in IoT Hub configuration.

Once the device is ready for the file ingestion, it uploads the file directly to the storage account in the container we selected. The IoT Hub gets a message about the file upload being completed through a file ingestion IoT Hub message and adds the notification.

An IoT backend application is responsible for downloading the file and processing the batch telemetry data that we just uploaded through the file.

There's more...

When a file is uploaded to blob storage from the IoT device; a `FileUploadNotification` message is posted in IoT Hub, the backend application can access a few more properties which are helpful while working on the backend application. The message has the property of the Blob URI, the Blob name, last updated time, and the size of the Blob in bytes.

Device firmware updates

The backend app is responsible for initiating a firmware update for the device through a direct method that it can run on the IoT device. The device then acts and downloads the firmware file, runs the firmware update, and finally reconnects to the IoT Hub service. Throughout the process, the IoT device uses the reported properties to update the progress and status of the device.

How to do it...

In this topic, we are going to create a C# simulator, which will use the device twin and direct methods to send the firmware update to device:

1. Create C# console IoT application.
2. Add a `Azure.Devices` package for NuGet.
3. Trigger the remote update to update the device firmware:

```
client =
ServiceClient.CreateFromConnectionString(AzureIoTHub.GetConnectionS
tring());
CloudToDeviceMethod method = new
CloudToDeviceMethod("firmwareUpdate");
method.ResponseTimeout = TimeSpan.FromSeconds(30);
method.SetPayloadJson(@"{fwPackageUri : '"+ bloburl + "'}");

CloudToDeviceMethodResult result = await
client.InvokeDeviceMethodAsync(targetDevice, method);
```

How it works...

This IoT backend solution has created a connection to call a direct method on the device side. It creates a connection using the `ServiceClient` object to invoke the `firmwareUpdate` method on the device side.

The `firmwareUpdate` method downloads the update image file and then applies it on the device to update the firmware. As soon as the firmware is updated, the device twin properties are updated, so the IoT backend application can query to it and check the reported properties, thus validating the updated status.

4
Azure IoT Communication Protocols

In this chapter, you will learn the following recipes:

- Hyper Text Transfer Protocol Secure (HTTPS)
- Advanced Message Queuing Protocol (AMQP)
- Using AMQP library to communicate with IoT Hub
- Message Queuing Telemetry Transport Protocol (MQTT)
- IoT protocol gateway
- Using MQTT .NET library to communicate with IoT Hub
- Connecting IoT Hub using MQTT client tools
- How to choose between protocols

Introduction

Accessing IoT Hubs is easy now that SDKs have been made available by Microsoft. These are open source and can be easily downloaded from GitHub. There are multiple language supports for using these SDKs. We will be using C# samples in this chapter to create a simulator and communicate with IoT Hub, followed by receiving these in another console's IoT solutions.

We can use HTTP, AMQP, or MQTT protocols. To connect with other platforms, we can use the protocol gateway that implements the custom communication; it is nothing but a framework. One of the options for implementing it is a cloud gateway, where we accept the data as a cloud service and then ingest it into the IoT Hub.

Hyper Text Transfer Protocol Secure (HTTPS)

HTTPS is one of the application protocols used for communicating between device-to-cloud and cloud-to-device. When you are using HTTP, devices poll IoT Hub for messages.

The HTTP protocol works for the command/response IoT system between the IoT device and the cloud application.

How to do it...

We will create a simulator and ingest data to IoT Hub:

1. Create a device simulator to send a message to the IoT:

```
deviceClient =
DeviceClient.CreateFromConnectionString("HostName=IoTHubCookBook.az
ure-
devices.net;DeviceId=myFirstDevice;SharedAccessKey=XXXXXXXXXXXXX",
TransportType.Http1);

new DeviceSimulator().SendDeviceToCloudMessagesAsync(deviceClient,
"myFirstDevice");
```

2. Send IoT Hub messages using HTTP:

```
public async void SendDeviceToCloudMessagesAsync(DeviceClient
deviceClient1, string deviceId) public async void
SendDeviceToCloudMessagesAsync(DeviceClient deviceClient1, string
deviceId)          {
            double avgWindSpeed = 10; // m/s
            Random rand = new Random();
            double currentWindSpeed = 0;
            int i = 0;
            while (i<10)
            {
                currentWindSpeed = avgWindSpeed + rand.NextDouble()
* 4 - 2;

                var telemetryDataPoint = new
                {
                    deviceId = deviceId,
                    windSpeed = currentWindSpeed,
                    highTemp = 72.3,
                    lowtemp = 11.2,
```

```
                          latitude = "17.5122560",
                          longitude = "70.7760470"
                  };
                  var messageString =
JsonConvert.SerializeObject(telemetryDataPoint);
                  var message = new
Message(Encoding.ASCII.GetBytes(messageString));
                  await deviceClient1.SendEventAsync(message);
                  i += 1;
                  await Task.Delay(1000);
              }
          }
```

3. Lets use the following code block to process the message ingested into IoT Hub:

```
readonly string iotHubD2cEndpoint = "messages/events";readonly
string iotHubD2cEndpoint = "messages/events";
eventHubClient =
EventHubClient.CreateFromConnectionString(AzureIoTHub.GetConnection
String(), iotHubD2cEndpoint);
var d2cPartitions =
eventHubClient.GetRuntimeInformation().PartitionIds;
          String data = "";
          foreach (string partition in d2cPartitions)
          {
              var result =
ReceiveMessagesFromDeviceAsync(partition);
              data = result.Result.ToString();
              if (data != "")
                  return data;
          }
 private async static Task<String>
ReceiveMessagesFromDeviceAsync(string partition)
      {
          var eventHubReceiver =
eventHubClient.GetDefaultConsumerGroup().CreateReceiver(partition,
DateTime.Now);
          while (true)
          {
              EventData eventData = await
eventHubReceiver.ReceiveAsync();
              if (eventData == null) continue;
              var data =
Encoding.UTF8.GetString(eventData.GetBytes());
              return data;
          }
      }
```

How it works...

IoT Hub SDK provides easy options to select between the communication protocols that we would like to make the device communicate with the IoT Hub cloud-based solutions. In this case, the simulator code is making use of IoT device SDKs to send the telemetry data using AMQP protocol. We need to define the transport type while making the connection. These SDKs will be required on the device side to be implemented to use the Azure IoT device SDK.

Once the IoT device gets connected with the IoT Hub and starts ingesting the data, it is available for IoT solution to pull these messages and process some data that could need to transformed before it proceeds further to the next step. Sometimes, it can be used through the stream analytics to provide real-time analytics on top of the data ingested.

 Microsoft Azure has launched a new service *Azure Time Series Analytics,* which is yet another powerful PaaS offering to work with time series data analytics.

Advanced Message Queuing Protocol (AMQP)

AMQP is considered to be a secure and reliable IoT protocol; it is also an advanced protocol. AMQP is mostly used in business messaging. AMQP works well for enterprise applications and server-to-server communication.

How to do it...

We will create a simulator application to ingest messages using AMQP protocol:

1. Create a device simulator to send a message to IoT Hub:

```
deviceClient =
DeviceClient.CreateFromConnectionString("HostName=IoTHubCookBook.az
ure-
devices.net;DeviceId=myFirstDevice;SharedAccessKey=XXXXXXXXXXXXX",
TransportType.Amqp);

new DeviceSimulator().SendDeviceToCloudMessagesAsync(deviceClient,
"myFirstDevice");
```

2. Send IoT Hub messages using AMQP:

```
public async void SendDeviceToCloudMessagesAsync(DeviceClient
deviceClient1, string deviceId) public async void
SendDeviceToCloudMessagesAsync(DeviceClient deviceClient1, string
deviceId)          {
            double avgWindSpeed = 10; // m/s
            Random rand = new Random();
            double currentWindSpeed = 0;
            int i = 0;
            while (i<10)
            {
                currentWindSpeed = avgWindSpeed + rand.NextDouble()
* 4 - 2;
                var telemetryDataPoint = new
                {
                    deviceId = deviceId,
                    windSpeed = currentWindSpeed,
                    highTemp = 72.3,
                    lowtemp = 11.2,
                    latitude = "17.5122560",
                    longitude = "70.7760470"
                };
                var messageString =
JsonConvert.SerializeObject(telemetryDataPoint);
                var message = new
Message(Encoding.ASCII.GetBytes(messageString));
                await deviceClient1.SendEventAsync(message);
                i += 1;
                await Task.Delay(1000);
            }
        }
```

3. Process the message ingested into IoT Hub:

```
readonly string iotHubD2cEndpoint = "messages/events";readonly
string iotHubD2cEndpoint = "messages/events";
eventHubClient =
EventHubClient.CreateFromConnectionString(AzureIoTHub.GetConnection
String(), iotHubD2cEndpoint);
var d2cPartitions =
eventHubClient.GetRuntimeInformation().PartitionIds;
            String data = "";
            foreach (string partition in d2cPartitions)
            {
                var result =
ReceiveMessagesFromDeviceAsync(partition);
                data = result.Result.ToString();
```

```
                     if (data != "")
                          return data;
                }
   private async static Task<String>
   ReceiveMessagesFromDeviceAsync(string partition)
         {
               var eventHubReceiver =
   eventHubClient.GetDefaultConsumerGroup().CreateReceiver(partition,
   DateTime.Now);
               while (true)
               {
                     EventData eventData = await
   eventHubReceiver.ReceiveAsync();
                     if (eventData == null) continue;
                     var data =
   Encoding.UTF8.GetString(eventData.GetBytes());
                     return data;
               }
         }
}
```

How it works...

IoT Hub SDK provides easy options to select between the protocols available. We would need to decide which protocol we like to use for device communication with IoT Hub. In this case, the simulator code is making use of IoT device SDKs to send the telemetry data using AMQP protocol. We need to define the transport type while making the connection. These IoT client SDKs will be required on the device side to be implemented to use the Azure IoT device SDKs.

Once the device gets connected with the hub and ingests the data, it is available for the IoT solution to pull this and process some data that could need to be transformed to proceed further. Sometimes it can be used through stream analytics to provide some real-time analytics using the data ingested by IoT device to IoT Hub.

Using AMQP library to communicate with IoT Hub

AMQP is a binary transfer protocol made for server-to-server communication, but nowadays, it is widely used in IoT solutions. Azure IoT SDK supports the AMQP communication protocol.

However, in this recipe, we will be using the `Amqp.Net Lite` library that provides an AMQP protocol stack written in C#. This can be used across multiple .NET-based platforms such as console or UWP applications.

Getting ready

IoT Hub expects secure connectivity with AMQP by making a connection over port `5671` when data is ingested from the device to the IoT Hub.

In this recipe, we will make a sender link and a receiver link. The sender will be used for telemetry data to the cloud and the receiver will be designed to accept the commands and process them.

How to do it...

We will use the AMQP library to implement using a AMQP protocol directly with IoT Hub:

1. Create a C# console application and add a class `amqpClient`.

2. Open the **Add new** NuGet packages and search for `AMQPNetLite`:

A Nuget package installer for AMQP

3. Declare the global variables:

```
string IoThubURI = "IoTHubCookBook.azure-devices.net";
int port = 5671;
```

4. We will create a `SendEvent` method which accepts the `deviceId` parameter.

5. Initialize the variables required for AMQP connection with IoT Hub:

```
string to = Fx.Format("/devices/{0}/messages/events", deviceId);
string entity = "/messages/events";
string audience = Fx.Format("{0}/devices/{1}", IoThubURI,
deviceId);
string resourceUri = Fx.Format("{0}/devices/{1}", IoThubURI,
deviceId);
string sasToken = "";//get shared signature from Device Explorer
bool cbs = PutCbsToken(connection, IoThubURI, sasToken, audience);
```

6. Connect AMQP session to start sending telemetry data:

```
session = new Session(connection);
SenderLink senderevent = new SenderLink(session, "senderevent",
to);
```

7. Once the connection is made, we will define our telemetry data point:

```
var telemetryDataPoint = new
        {
            deviceId = deviceId,
            windSpeed = currentWindSpeed,
            highTemp = 72.3,
            lowtemp = 11.2,
            latitude = "17.5122560",
            longitude = "70.7760470"
        };
```

8. Convert the data into JSON:

```
var json = JsonConvert.SerializeObject(telemetryDataPoint);
```

9. Now, publish the message:

```
var messageValue = Encoding.UTF8.GetBytes(json.ToString());
var telemetryMessage = new Message()
{
  BodySection = new Data() { Binary = messageValue }
};
senderevent.Send(telemetryMessage);
```

10. Read messages from the IoT Hub.
11. We will use the device explorer to read the messages published:

Configuration | Management | Data | Messages To Device | Call Method on Device

Monitoring

Event Hub: `IoTHubCookBook`

Device ID: `myFirstDevice`

Start Time: ☐ 07/10/2017 00:52:38

Consumer Group: $Default   ☐ Enable

[Monitor]   [Cancel]   [Clear]   ☐ Show system properties

Event Hub Data

2017-07-10 00:52:48> Device: [myFirstDevice], Data:
[{"deviceId":"myFirstDevice","windSpeed":9.79529626564835,"highTemp":72.3,"lowtemp":11.2,"latitude":"17.5122560","longitude":"70.7760470"}]
2017-07-10 00:52:49> Device: [myFirstDevice], Data:
[{"deviceId":"myFirstDevice","windSpeed":11.285766027535203,"highTemp":72.3,"lowtemp":11.2,"latitude":"17.5122560","longitude":"70.7760470"}]
2017-07-10 00:52:49> Device: [myFirstDevice], Data:
[{"deviceId":"myFirstDevice","windSpeed":10.020043059261536,"highTemp":72.3,"lowtemp":11.2,"latitude":"17.5122560","longitude":"70.7760470"}]
2017-07-10 00:52:49> Device: [myFirstDevice], Data:
[{"deviceId":"myFirstDevice","windSpeed":10.804629530201028,"highTemp":72.3,"lowtemp":11.2,"latitude":"17.5122560","longitude":"70.7760470"}]
2017-07-10 00:52:49> Device: [myFirstDevice], Data:
[{"deviceId":"myFirstDevice","windSpeed":11.553908323661382,"highTemp":72.3,"lowtemp":11.2,"latitude":"17.5122560","longitude":"70.7760470"}]

Device explorer tool reading window

12. Using the device explorer only, we will go to **Message to Device tab and send Message**:

Device explorer sending a cloud to device message

13. On the AMQP client console, we will create a new `ReceivedCommand` function to receive the messages from the IoT Hub:

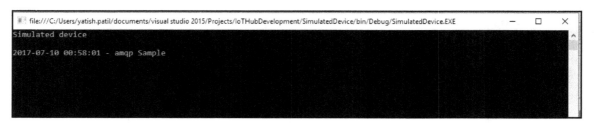

AMQP message read at device client

14. Initialize device connectivity with the IoT Hub and the device will post the messages to our AMQP client:

```
            string audience =
Fx.Format("{0}/messages/servicebound/feedback", IoThubURI);
            string resourceUri =
Fx.Format("{0}/messages/servicebound/feedback", IoThubURI);
  string entity = Fx.Format("/devices/{0}/messages/deviceBound",
"myFirstDevice");
            string returnString = "";
            string sasToken = "";//get shared signature from Device
Explorer
            bool cbs = PutCbsToken(connection, IoThubURI, sasToken,
audience);
            if (cbs)
            {
                session = new Session(connection);
            }
```

15. Let's connect the AMQP client with the IoT Hub:

```
ReceiverLink receiveCommand = new ReceiverLink(session,
"receiveCommand", entity);
```

16. Read the message and write to the console line:

```
received = receiveCommand.Receive();
            if (received != null)
            {
                receiveCommand.Accept(received);
                returnString =
Encoding.UTF8.GetString(received.GetBody<byte[]>());
                Console.WriteLine(returnString);
                // process the Command at Device
                // Write your code here
            }
receiveCommand.Close();
```

17. Now, from your `main` method of the console application, simply create the object of the `amqpClient` class and call the methods:

```
amqpClient clsamqpClient = new amqpClient();
            clsamqpClient.SendEvent("myFirstDevice");
            Thread receiverThread = new
Thread(clsamqpClient.ReceiveCommand);
            receiverThread.Start();
```

How it works...

This recipe, starts with create a Device simulator and connecting it by AMQP protocol to the IoT Hub. By default, all telemetry data goes in `/devices/{0}/messages/events`, and a shared access signature is generated using the device explorer tool.

To make this connectivity, we need to use the claim-based security token. Post that, we have created a sender link which sends all messages device-to-cloud.

In the latter part, we configured the receiver link to accept the command. We can even reject these using `Reject()` in a required scenario.

Using the device explorer tool, we can only view the communication and send a command back to the AMQP client that we have created. This will print it on the console. In the real world, we will process the command once it is accepted at the client side, which is an IoT device.

For more details on authentication and authorization using CBS, refer to the following link:

`https://docs.microsoft.com/en-us/azure/service-bus-messaging/service-bus-sas`

Message Queuing Telemetry Transport Protocol (MQTT)

MQTT targets device data collection. It is mainly used for telemetry, or remote monitoring purposes. MQTT collects data from many devices and transports that data to backend IoT services using publish and subscribe technique.

Getting started

Currently, IoT Hub offers two ways of implementing the MQTT protocol. The first option is to use the IoT Hub device SDK itself. This is suitable if you can easily write the code on the device side.

Secondly, you might face challenges in using IoT device SDK and writing the code on the device; especially if you have old devices in the fields. The solution is to use the MQTT protocol directly.

Let's try the option with IoT Hub device SDK first, and in the next section, we will go through another method.

How to do it...

Lets create a C# simulator which will send device-to-cloud message using MQTT protocol:

1. Create a device simulator to send a message to IoT Hub:

```
deviceClient =
DeviceClient.CreateFromConnectionString("HostName=IoTHubCookBook.az
ure-
devices.net;DeviceId=myFirstDevice;SharedAccessKey=XXXXXXXXXXXXX",
TransportType.Mqtt);

new DeviceSimulator().SendDeviceToCloudMessagesAsync(deviceClient,
"myFirstDevice");
```

2. Send IoT Hub messages using MQTT:

```
public async void SendDeviceToCloudMessagesAsync(DeviceClient
deviceClient1, string deviceId) public async void
SendDeviceToCloudMessagesAsync(DeviceClient deviceClient1, string
deviceId)         {
            double avgWindSpeed = 10; // m/s
            Random rand = new Random();
            double currentWindSpeed = 0;
            int i = 0;
            while (i<10)
            {
                currentWindSpeed = avgWindSpeed + rand.NextDouble()
* 4 - 2;
                var telemetryDataPoint = new
                {
                    deviceId = deviceId,
                    windSpeed = currentWindSpeed,
                    highTemp = 72.3,
                    lowtemp = 11.2,
                    latitude = "17.5122560",
                    longitude = "70.7760470"
                };
                var messageString =
JsonConvert.SerializeObject(telemetryDataPoint);
                var message = new
Message(Encoding.ASCII.GetBytes(messageString));
                await deviceClient1.SendEventAsync(message);
                i += 1;
                await Task.Delay(1000);
            }
        }
```

3. Process the message ingested into IoT Hub:

```
readonly string iotHubD2cEndpoint = "messages/events";readonly
string iotHubD2cEndpoint = "messages/events";
eventHubClient =
EventHubClient.CreateFromConnectionString(AzureIoTHub.GetConnection
String(), iotHubD2cEndpoint);
var d2cPartitions =
eventHubClient.GetRuntimeInformation().PartitionIds;
        String data = "";
        foreach (string partition in d2cPartitions)
        {
            var result =
ReceiveMessagesFromDeviceAsync(partition);
            data = result.Result.ToString();
            if (data != "")
                return data;
        }
 private async static Task<String>
ReceiveMessagesFromDeviceAsync(string partition)
        {
            var eventHubReceiver =
eventHubClient.GetDefaultConsumerGroup().CreateReceiver(partition,
DateTime.Now);
            while (true)
            {
                EventData eventData = await
eventHubReceiver.ReceiveAsync();
                if (eventData == null) continue;
                var data =
Encoding.UTF8.GetString(eventData.GetBytes());
                return data;
            }
        }
```

How it works...

The MQTT option is pretty much the same as the other protocols when using the IoT device SDKs. It requires the protocol type declaration at the start, when making the connection to the cloud.

Once established, the process remains the same as the other two protocols we looked at.

The message processing also the remains same as with the other protocols, as the IoT device simulator is ingesting the data to the message/events message route, which is the default queue with IoT Hub.

There's more...

Currently, MQTT does not support the reject operations when receiving cloud-to-device messages. If your scenarios need to handle such a rejection case, then you need to consider using direct methods.

A Direct method can be invoked on the Device side, it will perform the required action. in order to do so, we need to make sure that device understand and is capable of executing directing Methods.

IoT protocol gateway

HTTP, AMQP, and MQTT are the default protocols Azure IoT Hub supports for communication over the internet with devices or gateways. It could be possible that, in some scenarios, a few devices or field gateways might not be able to use one of these default protocols and will require protocol supports. In such cases, you can use a custom gateway. A custom gateway can enable a protocol wrapper for IoT Hub endpoints by bridging the traffic to and from IoT Hub, hence, avoiding any impact on your IoT implementation.

The Azure IoT protocol gateway is a framework for a protocol wrapper that is meant for scalable and bidirectional communication with IoT Hub.

Getting started

We will be creating a sample with which we will use the MQTT protocol to directly connect to the IoT Hub. The communication will be done using the public device endpoints for the MQTT protocol on port `8883`. In the simulator part, we will be using the MQTT `connect()` packet call to make the connection with the device.

How to do it...

In this section we are going to build the IoT protocol gateway:

1. Connection with IoT Hub:

```
{
  cmd: 'connect',
  protocolId: 'MQTT', // Or 'MQIsdp' in MQTT 3.1.1
  clean: true, // Can also be false
  clientId: 'myFirstDevice',          // Device Id registered in IoT
Hub
  keepalive: 0, // Seconds which can be any positive number, with 0
as the default setting
  username: 'IoTHubCookBook.azure-devices.net/myFirstDevice/api-
version=2016-11-14', // 'hostname/deviceId/version'
  password: 'LKCXsBKMKISTjr3ii08UXgIpELxy8/38EiMuxNAiqek=', //
SharedAccessKey
  will: {
    topic: 'devices/myFirstDevice/messages/events/'
  }
}
```

2. Process the message ingested into IoT Hub:

```
readonly string iotHubD2cEndpoint = "messages/events";readonly
string iotHubD2cEndpoint = "messages/events";
eventHubClient =
EventHubClient.CreateFromConnectionString(AzureIoTHub.GetConnection
String(), iotHubD2cEndpoint);
var d2cPartitions =
eventHubClient.GetRuntimeInformation().PartitionIds;
            String data = "";
            foreach (string partition in d2cPartitions)
            {
                var result =
ReceiveMessagesFromDeviceAsync(partition);
                data = result.Result.ToString();
                if (data != "")
                    return data;
            }
 private async static Task<String>
ReceiveMessagesFromDeviceAsync(string partition)
        {
                var eventHubReceiver =
eventHubClient.GetDefaultConsumerGroup().CreateReceiver(partition,
DateTime.Now);
                while (true)
```

```
        {
                EventData eventData = await
eventHubReceiver.ReceiveAsync();
                if (eventData == null) continue;
                var data =
Encoding.UTF8.GetString(eventData.GetBytes());
                return data;
        }
    }
```

How it works...

The protocol gateway gets deployed in Azure in a scalable way by using Azure Cloud Services or Azure Service Fabric, or we can even use the Windows VM. In a scenario, it can be deployed in on-premise environments, such as field gateways.

Once the message gets into the IoT Hub, it works in the same way. Our IoT backend application will read messages from the IoT Hub and process those accordingly. we can use the C# application we created in `Chapter 3`, *IoT Hub Messaging and Commands*. This application will read the messages from IoT hub and process it.

There's more...

While using MQTT protocol directly to connect and disconnect packets, additional information is issued by IoT Hub-an event on the operations monitoring channel. Using this, one can troubleshoot connectivity issues.

Using MQTT .NET library to communicate with IoT Hub

MQTT is a **Machine-to-Machine (M2M)** client server publish/subscribe messaging transport protocol. It is a lightweight, low-bandwidth, high-latency network, and easy to implement connectivity protocol.

The key benefits of MQTT protocol are:

- Simple to implement
- Provide **Quality of Service (QoS)** data delivery
- Lightweight and bandwidth efficient

MQTT protocol can connects multiple devices using the publish/subscribe mechanism to collect data from many devices. The MQTT, targets device data collection mainly for telemetry or remote monitoring purposes. It then transports that data to the backend central system using publish/subscribe mechanism.

In this recipe, we will understand the MQTT protocol and will create a C# console application using M2MQTT library to connect to the IoT Hub and ingest the data.

Getting ready

If M2M connectivity exist, the device may not be able to use the IoT Hub SDK. But with MQTT support added to the IoT Hub, a public endpoint can be used to connect.

MQTT protocol has the following main components:

Client: The MQTT client is any device that has the MQTT library and is capable of connecting to the broker to publish or subscribe the messages via the available topics. MQTT library is also available in different languages. We have used M2MQTT for the console application, which is also available through the NuGet package installer.

Broker: The broker is the central system between two different devices. Its job is to receive all the messages from the publishing clients and send them to the subscribing clients. The broker is also responsible for the authentication and authorization of clients. It is important for highly-scalable systems, as in case of failure, it can be a bottleneck. Hence, it needs to be designed considering these failure scenarios as well. There are commercial implementations of MQTT brokers such as HiveMQ and a few more.

Topic: Topics are simple. They are hierarchical strings to filter messages for each connected client. A forward slash is used as a delimiter to maintain this separation.

Examples of topic are:

- home/ac/livingroom/temperature
- office/ac/meetingroom/temperature

How to do it...

lets create a console application using a MQTT library:

1. Create a C# console application and add a class `mqttClient`.
2. Open the Add new NuGet packages and search for `M2Mqtt`:

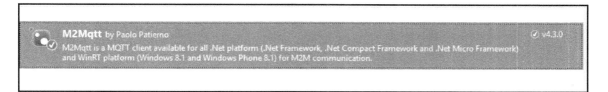

MQTT NuGet package installer

3. Declare the global variables:

   ```
   MqttClient client;
   string IoThubURI = "IoTHubCookBook.azure-devices.net";
   int MqttPort = 8883;
   ```

4. We will create a method `SendEvent`, which accepts `deviceId` and `device Key` parameters.

5. Initialize the variables required for MQTT connection with IoT Hub:

   ```
   string target = string.Format("{0}/devices/{1}", IoThubURI,
   deviceId);
   string Username = string.Format("{0}/{1}", IoThubURI, deviceId);
   string Password = CreateSharedAccessSignature(deviceId, deviceKey,
   target);
   ```

6. Create a MQTT client instance by initiating the `MqttClient` class:

   ```
   client = new MqttClient(IoThubURI, MqttPort, true,
   MqttSslProtocols.TLSv1_0, (sender, certificate, chain, errors) =>
   true, null);
               client.Connect(deviceId, Username, Password);
   ```

7. Once the connection is made, we will define our telemetry data point:

   ```
   var telemetryDataPoint = new
   {
       deviceId = deviceId,
       windSpeed = currentWindSpeed,
   ```

```
highTemp = 72.3,
lowtemp = 11.2,
latitude = "17.5122560",
longitude = "70.7760470"
};
```

8. Convert the data into JSON:

```
var json = JsonConvert.SerializeObject(telemetryDataPoint);
```

9. Now publish the message:

```
client.Publish(string.Format("devices/{0}/messages/events/telemetry
", deviceId),
Encoding.UTF8.GetBytes(JsonConvert.SerializeObject(json)));
```

10. Read messages from the IoT Hub.

11. Device explorer is a tool which helps in quickly managing the Devices and operations with IoT Hub. We will be looking into details of using this tool in `Chapter 9`, *Managing the Azure IoT Hub*.

12. we can install this tool from `https://github.com/Azure/azure-iot-sdks/rele ases`. File name is `SetupDeviceExplorer.msi`.

13. We will use the device explorer to read the messages published:

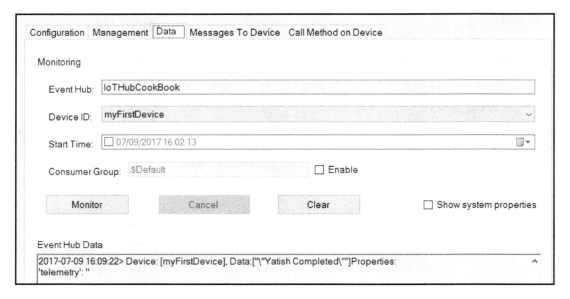

Device-to-cloud message using MQTT

14. Using the device explorer tool, we can send messages from the **Message to Device** tab:

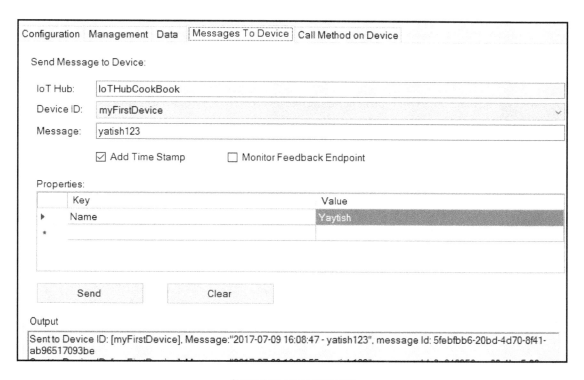

Cloud-to-device message using MQTT

15. On the MQTT client console, we will create a new `ReceivedCommand` function to subscribe to the messages from the IoT Hub.

16. Initialize the topic that the IoT Hub will post the messages on, and our MQTT client needs to subscribe for:

```
string target =
string.Format("{0}/devices/{1}/messages/devicebound/#", IoThubURI,
deviceId);
string Username = string.Format("{0}/{1}", IoThubURI, deviceId);
string Password = CreateSharedAccessSignature(deviceId, deviceKey,
target);
```

17. Let's connect the MQTT client with the IoT Hub:

```
client = new MqttClient(IoThubURI, MqttPort, true,
MqttSslProtocols.TLSv1_0, (sender, certificate, chain, errors) =>
true, null);
```

18. Define the event handler to process the received command at MQTT client:

```
client.MqttMsgSubscribed += client_MqttMsgSubscribed;
client.MqttMsgPublishReceived += client_MqttMsgPublishReceived;
```

19. Now you can subscribe for multiple topics as follows:

```
client.Subscribe(new string[] { target}, new byte[] {
MqttMsgBase.QOS_LEVEL_EXACTLY_ONCE});
client.Subscribe(new string[] { "/#" }, new byte[] {
MqttMsgBase.QOS_LEVEL_EXACTLY_ONCE });
```

20. The `CreateSharedAccessSignature` method creates the shared access signature based on the device ID, device key, and topic path for that telemetry message:

```
return new SharedAccessSignatureBuilder
{
    Key = deviceKey,
    Target = target,
    KeyName = null,
    TimeToLive = TimeSpan.FromMinutes(20)
}.ToSignature();
```

21. Now from your `main` method of console the application, simply create the object of `mqttClient` class and call the methods:

```
mqttClient clsmqttClient = new mqttClient();
clsmqttClient.SendEvent("myFirstDevice",
"LKCXsBKMKISTjr3ii08UXgIpELxy8/38EiMuxNAiqek=");
clsmqttClient.RecievedCommand("myFirstDevice",
"LKCXsBKMKISTjr3ii08UXgIpELxy8/38EiMuxNAiqek=");
```

How it works...

First, we will establish the connectivity with Azure IoT Hub. We will need to use the host URL, device ID, and key, along with the topic. Once we are connected, we will be sending the data to `"devices/{0}/messages/events/telemetry"`.

The second part of this recipe is to receive the command at MQTT client. The topic used for this purpose is "`devices/{0}/messages/devicebound/#`".

Using the device explorer tool, we can read the messages ingested into the IoT Hub through this MQTT client and, also using the same tool, we can send some messages back to the client.

There's more...

You can refer to detailed documentation and the latest releases and updates for MQTT protocol at `http://mqtt.org/`.

M2MQTT, version for .NET based development, is available at `https://m2mqtt.wordpress.com/`.

NuGet package library to download the MQTT library is: `https://www.nuget.org/packages/M2Mqtt/`.

Connecting IoT Hub using MQTT client tools

In this recipe, we will use a `MQTTBox` tool as the MQTT client. So, instead of creating code-based application, we will be using a tool to establish connectivity with the IoT Hub and then create the publisher, as well as subscribe to send and receive data respectively.

Getting ready

We will download the Windows-based installer and configure the `MQTTBox` tool. Also, we will need the device explorer tool, which we can use to generate the shared secure keys or to send any data to the MQTT client.

Basically, this tool is nothing but a simulator in place of a real device connecting over MQTT protocol. This way, we can test the connectivity with the IoT Hub and send some dummy data to verify any connectivity issues and resolve them.

How to do it...

Lets configure and use MQTT client tool:

1. Download and install the `MQTTBox` tool from `http://workswithweb.com/html/mqttbox/downloads.html`.

2. Click on the **Create MQTT Client** to create a new connection:

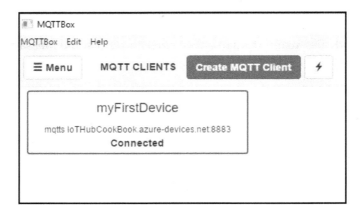

MQTT client connection

3. Configure the MQTT Client:

```
MQTT Client Name = myFirstmqttclient
MQTT Client Id = 'myFirstDevice'
HOST: IoTHubCookBook.azure-devices.net:8883
username: IoTHubCookBook.azure-devices.net/{Device
Id}/DeviceClientType=azure-iot-device%2F1.1.0-dtpreview&api-
version=2016-11-14
password: Genreate SharedAccessSignature using Device explorer
Append timestamp to MQTT client Id = NO
```

4. Click `Publish` – you should get a green connected status. Send telemetry data to the topic:

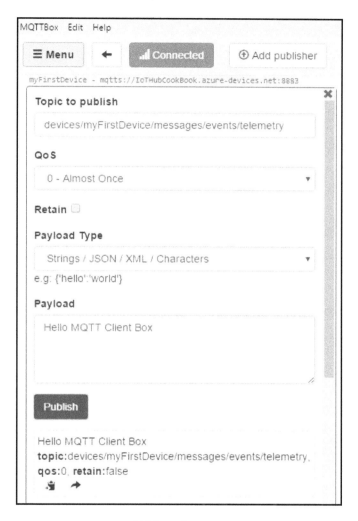

Publishing a MQTT message

5. Read data in the device explorer:

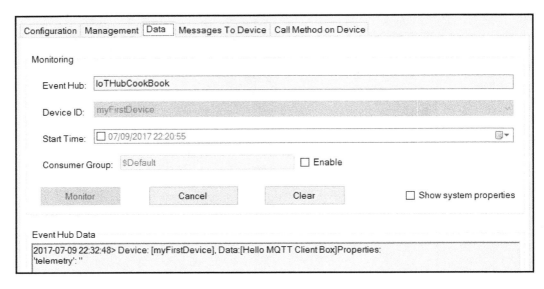

Receiving message in device explorer

6. Subscribe to the MQTT client to receive messages:

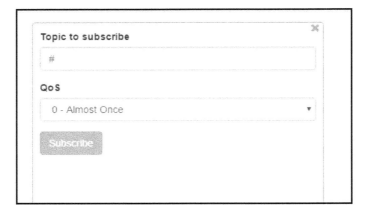

Subscribe the MQTT client tool

7. Send data from the device explorer:

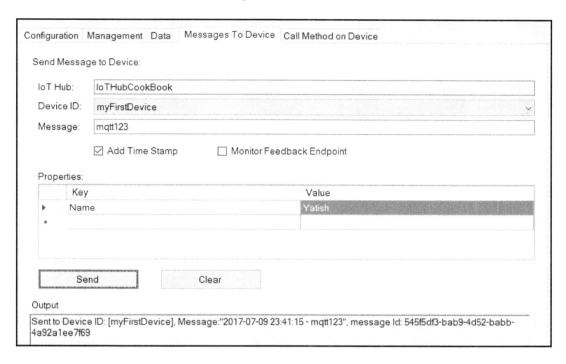

Send cloud-to-device message

8. Subscribe and receive data in the MQTTBox client:

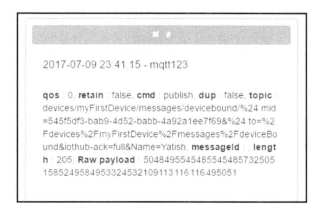

Message received in MQTT client tool

How it works...

The MQTTBox tool provides a simulator which helps us connect to the IoT Hub and publish messages at the same time as subscribing for cloud-to-device messages.

The client settings require the connectivity configuration. Once all settings are in place, it will automatically connect with the host, which we provide in the settings.

In the topic to publish, we need to mention the path `'devices/{device name}/messages/events/{Topic Name}'`. Apart from this, we can set the QoS and provide the actual data in the payload.

Using the device explorer, we read the data from IoT Hub. Instead of this, we can even write our own console application and make use of it.

Using the device explorer only, we can send the command to the MQTT client and that can be received by the tool by subscribing to the correct topics.

How to choose between protocols

Azure IoT Hub currently supports three different protocols. All of them work differently and are implemented in IoT solutions depending on the needs of the communication from the device to IoT Hub.

Getting ready

First, let's recap the three protocols, HTTP, MQTT, AMQP. MQTT protocol works on a publish and subscribe architecture. A MQTT client subscribes to a channel on a server, and when a server receives new information for that channel, it pushes it out to that device.

MQTT provides the QoS feature, which defines the priority for the communication between the device and server. These are:

- 0: deliver the message once
- 1: deliver the message at least once
- 2: deliver the message exactly once

The AMQP is another session layer protocol that runs over TCP and provides a publish/subscribe architecture which is like that of MQTT.

The difference between AMQP and MQTT is that AMQP creates multiple queues for the subscribers to receive the message. These messages are the telemetry data sent by the publisher.

The message broker supports clients connecting with the HTTP protocol using a REST API. However, HTTP does not have an efficient way to implement the server push, so when you implement HTTP protocol communication for IoT devices you need to poll the cloud-to-device messages from IoT Hub.

Currently with HTTP protocol, each device should poll for messages every 25 minutes or more, which is not the case with the others; they can push messages while receiving.

While designing your IoT solution you should compare these protocols. Let's consider questions which we need to answer to choose the protocol to use for your IoT solution.

How do it...

Lets ask few questions that will help us the need for specific protocol for our solution:

- Does your IoT device work on request and response architecture? This question defines the one way or bidirectional communication is required or not for your solution.

    HTTPs would be a good protocol to implement your IoT solution

- Does your IoT device need to run a long active process? It means the connected operation that you want to automate will need more time to finish.

    HTTPs would be a good protocol to implement your IoT solution

- Does your IoT device collect data from various end sensors? The end device connectivity will establish the need for protocol selection.

    MQTT would be a good protocol to implement your IoT solution

- If you are connecting M2M devices:

    MQTT would be a good protocol to implement your IoT solution

- If you need reliable routing of messages:

AMQP support reliable queuing and flexible routing.

How it works...

There is no best protocol in IoT; the use case is what defines which protocol should be considered, as IoT is a very vast protocol and they each solve some or the other use cases.

There are basically three kinds of connections:

- Device-to-device connectivity
- Device-to-service connectivity
- Service-to-service connectivity

The MQTT protocol works on publish /subscribe architecture, in which the MQTT broker relates to multiple devices, which on a set interval publishes the messages, and a subscriber through this broker receives the messages. So, the MQTT is used in device-to-device connectivity user cases.

AMQP is nothing but a queuing system designed to connect multiple servers to each other. AMQP uses the routing of messages in different queues, making it service-to-service connectivity. Services are set to their respective queues configured by exchange. It also helps in load balancing queues; the smallest packet size can be 60 bytes.

Whereas HTTP works on a request and response basis, any IoT device that uses the HTTP protocol needs to pull messages from the IoT Hub. It does not implement QoS like MQTT or AMQP. Security can be implemented using the **Secured Socket Layer (SSL) / Transport Layer Security (TLS)** connection.

5
Azure IoT Hub Security and Best Practices

In this chapter, you will learn following recipes:

- Securing a device with IoT Hub
- Securing a communication
- IP filtering with IoT Hub
- IoT Hub access rights
- Security best practices

Introduction

The era of the **Internet of Things** (**IoT**) is growing at a tremendous pace. Digitally connected devices are innovated for every aspect of our lives, including our homes, offices, cars, and our bodies too; with researchers claiming that, by 2020, the number of active wireless connected devices will exceed 40 billion.

It's up to the manufacturer and the system implementer of these IoT devices and IoT solutions to use more effective methods of IoT security in the following four areas:

- **IoT devices**: Devices which can capture and send telemetry data to the cloud.
- **Field gateway**: Devices that can aggregate data to and from the end devices which are unable to connect directly, this could be due to limitations such as protocol communication and so on.

- **Cloud gateways**: Any cloud endpoint that is able to receive data or send commands to field gateways or IoT devices out in the field.
- **Cloud services**: User services such as web applications or mobile applications that consume data received from IoT devices and takes action or controls the IoT devices.

In the IoT industry, there has been quite a lot of talk between manufacturers, users, and the experts about security concerns. Many businesses are constantly expanding their data sources and increasing their productivity and monitoring assets. We, as consumers, are responsible for using the best security practices available with the IoT solution and platform.

As device data moving from one zone to another needs to be secure, Microsoft Azure provides security for IoT deployment. This also includes the **STRIDE** model - Spoofing, Tampering, Repudiation, Information disclosure, Denial of service and Elevation of access permissions. The best way to make sure your application is secure is by considering threat modelling during the design/implementation phase of your IoT solution.

Microsoft Azure IoT makes it quick and easy to securely connect your IoT devices to the cloud. The following diagram shows how IoT suite considers the security aspect:

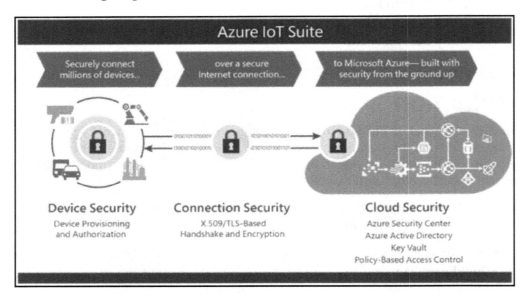

Securing a device with IoT Hub

IoT Hub provides hyper-scale identity registry for millions of devices per unit. The Azure IoT Hub secures devices while they are out in the field by registering them in Hub and providing a unique identity key for each IoT device. These secured details require the IoT solution/backend application to communicate with the device while it is in the field operation. It is a quick and easy process to configure an IoT device which can communicate over the internet into the IoT Hub. The device manufacturer will associate these details during the manufacturing of the hardware unless an **Over the AIR (OTA)** technique is implemented.

Getting ready

The Azure IoT SDKs help to manage any devices that are a part of the IoT Hub. Each IoT device, when registered in the IoT Hub unit, gets a unique device ID and a key generated for it. The identity registry provides secure storage of device identities and security keys for an IoT solution.

How to do it...

Let's use the device explorer to manage the devices:

1. Download the tool from the following link:

   ```
   https://github.com/Azure/azure-iot-sdk-csharp/tree/master/tools/Devi
   ceExplorer
   ```

2. Connect with the IoT Hub:

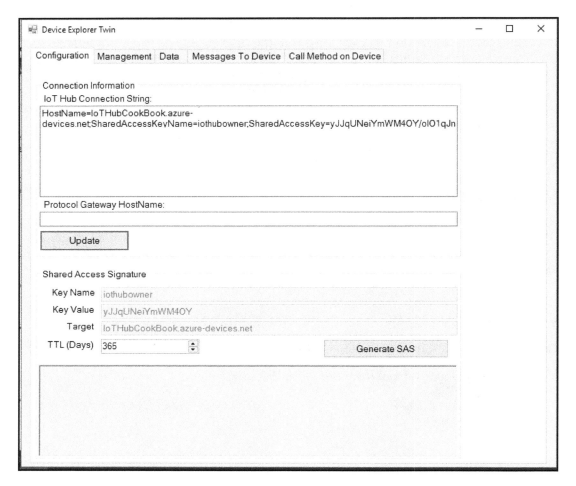

Device explorer connecting with IoT Hub

3. In the **Management** tab, we will find all the IoT devices associated with this Hub unit:

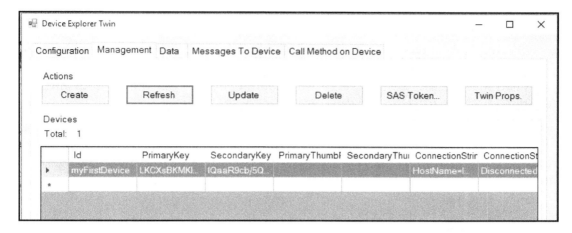

List of devices

4. Now, let's create a new device and generate a new set of secure keys:

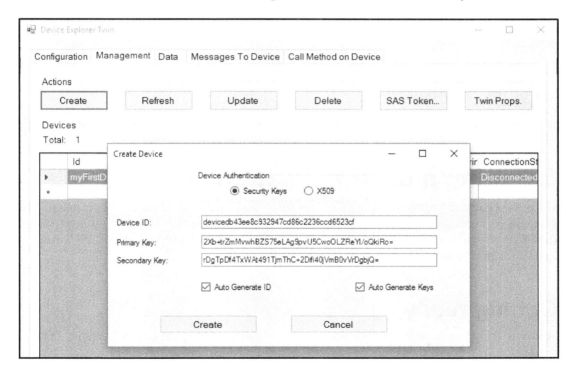

Create a new device

How it works...

We just followed one of the ways in which we can create devices, but the security of those devices is what we are looking at. You will notice that the device ID and secure key generated for devices is unique across the millions of devices that are out in the field and registered with the IoT Hub. We can control secure keys with auto generate options as well.

Azure IoT Hub access control policies in the cloud enable the management of any device identity, providing a way to control a device from an IoT deployment as and when required. This managing of devices is based on each device identity, which is registered in the hub securely.

There's more...

There are multiple ways to register or manage a device in the IoT Hub, right from the command-line tool to the device explorer tool for the IoT Hub. The Windows IoT core dashboard can also be used to register a new device or manage existing ones. We used the IoT Hub SDK in `Chapter 2`, *Introducing Device Management,* to create or manage an IoT device.

 The unique device ID stored in the identity registry is case sensitive.

Securing a communication

With the estimated number of IoT devices set to increase in the coming years across the globe, it is important how we connect those devices. The durability of receiving telemetry data from devices and delivering commands in response will be an important feature of any IoT solution which needs to be considered.

Getting ready

Azure IoT Hub does not permit insecure connections. **Transport Layer Security** (**TLS**) is always enforced. All messages are tagged with the originator on the service side, allowing the detection of in-payload origin spoofing attempts.

The Azure IoT Hub SDK provides a messaging infrastructure to establish secure communication between the connected devices using several IoT protocols such as HTTPS, MQTT, and AMQPS. **HTTP Secure (HTTPS)** is one of the industry-standard secure versions of the popular HTTP protocol, and is supported by Azure IoT Hub, thus enabling efficient communication.

There are some **Advanced Message Queuing Protocol (AMQP)** and **Message Queuing Telemetry Transport (MQTT)** protocols supported by Azure IoT Hub, which are designed not only for efficiency in terms of resource use, but also reliable message delivery between the IoT Hub and IoT devices over the internet. Azure IoT Hub enables secure connection to both IP-enabled and non-IP-enabled devices.

How to do it...

Using IoT Hub SDK, we will look at methods for secure communication:

1. Create a simulator device or IoT gateway using IoT Hub SDK.
2. Define the connection using one of the protocols supported by IoT Hub:

```
DeviceClient.CreateFromConnectionString("HostName=IoTHubCookBook.az
ure-  devices.net;DeviceId=myFirstDevice;SharedAccessKey= ",
TransportType.Mqtt)
```

3. The different `TransportType` supported are:

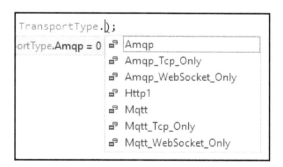

List of communication protocol

There's more...

Some devices connect only over short distance communication protocols, such as Z-wave, ZigBee, and Bluetooth. In these scenarios, a field gateway is used to collect the data from these devices and perform protocol translation to enable secure bidirectional communication with the cloud end that is the IoT Hub.

Some additional features that Microsoft provides are:

- Communication between devices and Azure IoT Hub, or between gateways and Azure IoT Hub, is secured through encryption technologies such as TLS and X.509 protocol as per industry standards.
- Azure IoT Hub does not open any connections to the device. The device initiates all connections.
- Azure IoT Hub durably stores messages for devices and waits for the device to connect.

IP filtering with IoT Hub

Security is an important aspect of any IoT solution based on the Azure IoT Hub. Sometimes, your IoT solution needs to explicitly give the range of the IP addresses from which the devices can connect as part of the custom IoT security configuration. IP filtering enables customers to configure IoT Hub to only accept connections from specific IP addresses assigned to the IoT devices or to block communication for a specific range of IP addresses.

Getting ready

The IP filter configuration is very easy for an administrator. These rules apply any time a device or a backend application connects on any supported protocols (currently AMQP, MQTT, AMQP/WS, MQTT/WS, HTTP/1).

> The IP filter allows a maximum 10 rules each, rejecting or accepting an IP range that can be specified in the IoT Hub configuration.

How to do it...

Using the Azure portal, we will configure the IoT Hub for IP filtering:

1. Log in to the Azure portal and navigate to the IoT Hub blade.

2. See the default settings:

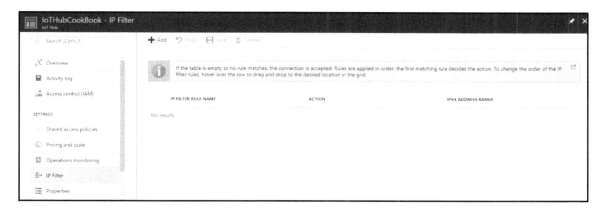

Navigate to Azure portal and IoT Hub service

3. Create a rejection rule:

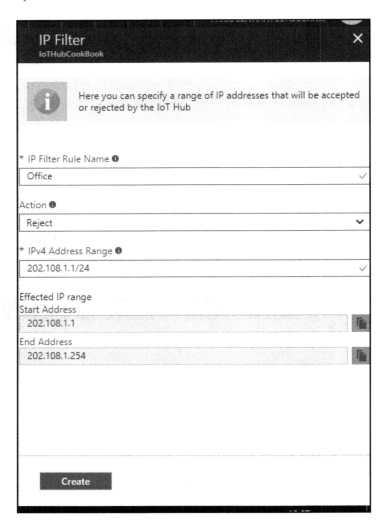

Configure the rule

4. Delete the existing rule:

Delete IP filtering rule

How it works...

The IP filter rule is applied at the IoT Hub service level. The rule office that we created in the preceding steps will apply to all connections from devices and backend IoT applications.

When an IP address in the rejected list tries to connect, the IoT Hub throws a 401 unauthorized code exception.

If you have multiple rules specified, they get applied in the order it gets listed in the grid.

You can change the rules order in which you would like to execute for communicating devices or backend services.

There's more...

When you create the IoT Hub unit, the IP filter grid shows empty. This means that your hub will accept connections from any IP address or IoT devices. This configuration is equivalent to a subnet rule which falls within the 0.0.0.0/0 IP address range. You can define the subnet range or you can define the exact IP address; both work in the same way.

IoT Hub access rights

IoT Hub has a defined set of permissions that needs to be taken into consideration. It is used for any IoT device or backend solution to connect or communicate with the IoT Hub. Once you have the appropriate permission, only then you will be able to access the respective IoT Hub endpoints.

Getting ready

The different permissions that you can grant to a device or backend application to access your IoT Hub are:

- **iothubowner**: This will allow any device or backend solution all permissions
- **service**: This will allow an access policy with only the **Service connect** permission
- **device**: This will enable the device with an access Policy which has the **Device connect** permission
- **registryRead**: This is a policy with **Registry read** permission
- **registryReadWrite**: This is a policy with **Registry read** and **Registry write** permissions
- Per-device security credentials: Each device's credentials are maintained in the device registry

How to do it...

This recipe will guide you through different access permissions that IoT Hub provides:

1. To provide full control over the IoT Hub, we need to use the **iothubowner** connection.

2. In the **Shared access keys,** we will use one of the existing options:

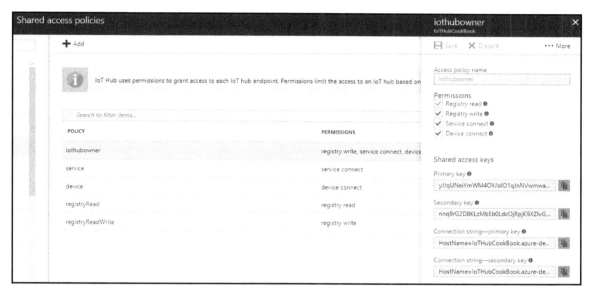

IoT Hub access permission

3. We can even define a new policy, which can be a combination of the default policies provided by IoT Hub, which are listed in the following screenshot:

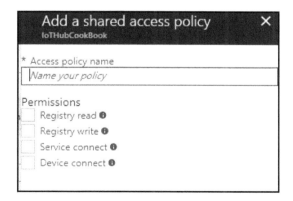

Access policy list

How it works...

If you want an administrator user to manage the device management component, the access permission of IoT Hub that user requires is the **registryReadWrite** policy. The backend solution will require the **Service connect** policy to access the IoT Hub information.

The authentication of the IoT Hub for each endpoint is based on the access policy permission that the incoming request has. Each communication protocol has their own ways to connect or establish a connectivity with the IoT Hub and pass the required information. For example, HTTPS uses a header to send across the shared keys and token details.

These tokens follow the security architecture guidelines for IoT Hub. In the case of IoT devices, the symmetric key stored in the device registry is used for communication, while the IoT solution uses the shared access policy.

Security best practices

The IoT security strategy defines how to secure data in the cloud and protect data integrity, while IoT device telemetry data does the communication over the public internet, and securely provisions IoT devices which are continuously running and collecting data in the field. One needs to work on this strategy from the manufacturing, development, and deployment of IoT devices and their implementation infrastructure.

How to do it...

In this recipe we will try to use the security practices:

1. Design the hardware such that it should be operational for the minimum required activity and time. Some IoT devices are battery-powered and can live a long life if this strategy is followed.
2. Tampering with the device in the field is critical. While designing the concept of any IoT device, how it can be tamper-free needs to be considered. One could have an event or alarm raised when a device is physically handled.

3. Any IoT device upgrade should be done in a secure way. This could be through physically travelling to a location and manually updating it through a secure application that is under the control of selected field engineers. Another way could be over-the-air upgrades.

4. While an IoT solution is being developed, it needs to be implemented on the security parameter standard defined at its implementation, testing, and deployment stages. Today, there are many choices for protocols, platforms, and technology.

5. The integration of software and hardware needs to be done carefully, because the exchange of data happens at this layer only.

6. After every time period, an audit should take place to check the health of the devices or solutions implemented.

There's more...

Azure Security Center provides a unified dashboard with security information on top of your existing Azure resources. This gives insights into which resources are vulnerable or detect events that were undetected in the past. Alongside that, the service also heavily analyzes all the data and uses machine learning to improve the detection system. This could be crucial for any large IoT implementation.

Apart from this, Microsoft also has a security program for Azure IoT. This program provides a set of best-in-class security auditors which the IoT implementer can choose from to perform a security audit on their IoT solutions, find issues, and provide recommendations.

6
IoT Suite and Pre-Configured Solutions

In this chapter, we will learn the following recipes:

- Creating a pre-configured solution
- IoT Suite remote monitoring
- IoT Suite predictive maintenance
- IoT Suite connected factory
- Customizing an IoT Suite

Introduction

Many IoT implementations fail to go live on production quickly for their users. There could be multiple reasons for this. Microsoft Azure is providing an accelerator to overcome this with a collection of Azure services that enable you to capture and analyze the data generated by your business. This is known as the Azure IoT Suite. Using this, one can accelerate the time to value with pre-configured solutions and move from **Proof of Concept** (**PoC**) to the broader idea of deployment.

The Azure IoT Suite gives enterprises an easy and seamless way to connect people, devices, and assets. It connects a broad range of devices and operating systems. These IoT devices will send that telemetry data to the Azure IoT backend using the Azure IoT Hub device SDK. If devices cannot communicate directly to the IoT Hub, this issue can be solved by using the cloud gateway or intermediate gateway to collect the data and then forward it to the IoT Hub. The IoT solution backend receives, transforms, processes, and stores the data into suitable storage. The Power BI enables presenting data in the form of dashboard reports.

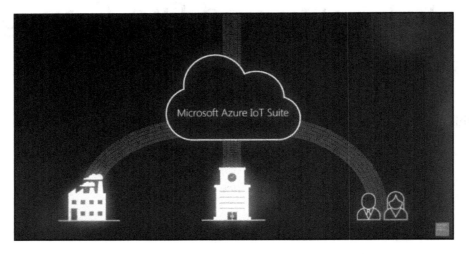

Image from Microsoft Azure IoT Suite documentation

The IoT Suite does offers customization of the pre-configured solutions. This will help you to fit the unique needs of organization's solutions. It provides finished applications to speed the deployment of common scenarios that we come across in many industries, like remote monitoring, asset management and predictive maintenance, and newly added connected factories. These solutions have the ability to grow and scale solutions to millions of things. Each pre-configured solution is a complete, end-to-end implementation that uses simulated devices to generate telemetry data.

Creating a Pre-configured solution

This recipe will help you understand how you can provision a pre-configured IoT Suite solution and what are the common scenarios available. The pre-configured solutions can be created using the link: https://www.azureiotsuite.com/.

Getting ready

To access the Azure IoT Suite portal, you will need to have Azure service administrator access. We will look into the currently available pre-configured solutions and the services which are part of the suite gets created.

 You can refer to the following link to manage other roles and allow them to create solutions.

https://docs.microsoft.com/en-us/azure/iot-suite/iot-suite-per missions#azure-subscription-administrator-roles

How to do it...

In this section we will see how to create IoT Suite solution,:

1. Log in to https://www.azureiotsuite.com/.

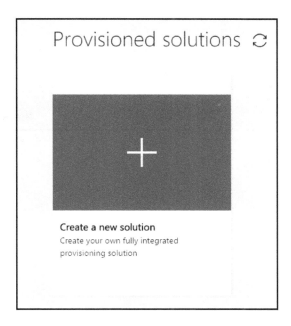

2. You must click on the + sign to see the currently available solutions:

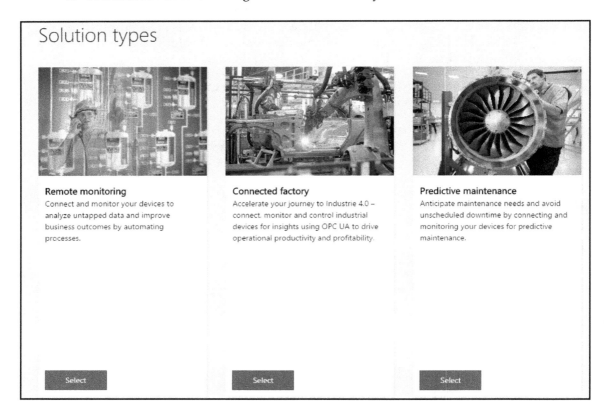

3. Once you select a solution and deploy it in your Azure subscription, it works in the background and in a few minutes it gets deployed:

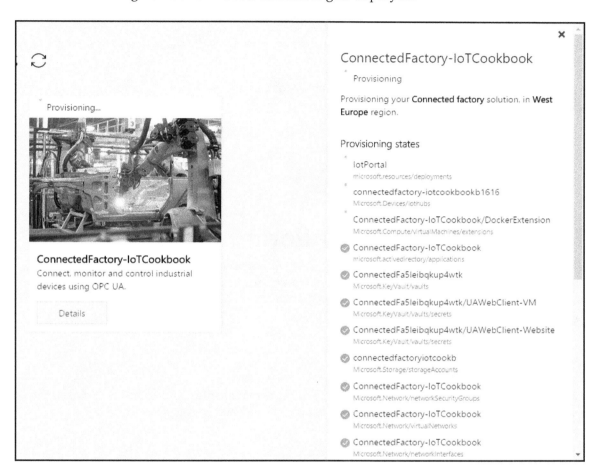

How it works...

The azureiotsuite.com provides an easy way to create pre-configured solutions. Once you log in with the appropriate access rights, it gives you the details of the existing solutions if any, or you can create new solutions with small descriptions about the solution.

To select the pre-configured solution you need to first find out the similarities of your business scenarios with IoT Suite options, and if required, it can be customized also. Once you provision pre-Configured solution, it automatically creates other required Azure services in the same resource group. all these services are deployed with some set of pre defined configuration. They occurs charges as per their configuration. it is very important to understand the Services part of this Solution and their pricing.

Let's follow the next few recipes in this chapter to create these solutions and then see how to customize them!

 You can delete the pre-configured solutions from the existing solution dashboard on the website, `Azureiotsuite.com`

IoT Suite remote monitoring

The remote monitoring solution is a common business scenario of an end-to-end monitoring of remotely deployed devices. It brings multiple IoT services together which includes, IoT Hub, stream analytics, web applications, event hub, Azure storage, DocumentDB, and Power BI dashboard.

Getting ready

Let's understand the architecture behind the remote monitoring solution; this architecture is published by Microsoft and depicts the Azure services used in this solution:

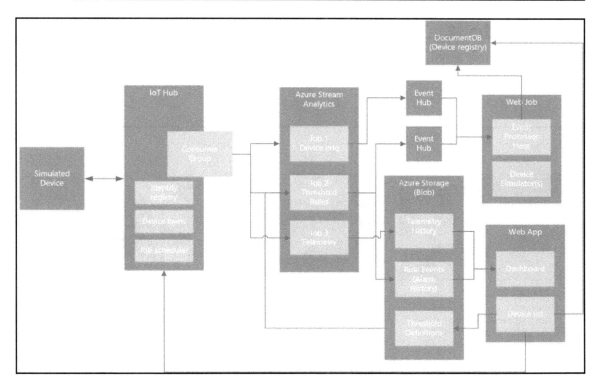

Remote monitoring suite architecture given by Microsoft Azure

The remote monitoring solution uses a simulated device to ingest the data into the IoT Hub. The simulated devices are already configured into the IoT Hub, we just need to start the devices to enable them to ingest the data. In this scenario, the IoT Hub is also used to send the commands, schedule jobs, direct method, and so on.

A stream analytics service is used for three different purposes, the first one being device info, which filters device information messages from the incoming message stream and sends them to an event hub endpoint.

Another job, called rules, checks all the incoming temperature and humidity values for the threshold configured from the dashboard portal. The alarms are set based on this data.

The third job is used for telemetry purposes. It inserts data into the storage. The aggregates done on this data are then displayed on the charts.

The event processor host processes the data which is inserted into the event hub from the device info and rules jobs. This event processor runs in the web job.

How to do it...

lets create a remote monitoring solution:

1. To create a remote monitoring solution, navigate to the following site: `azureiotsuite.com`.

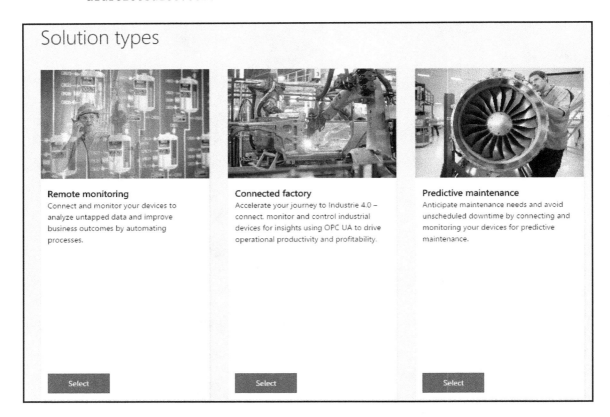

2. Provide the required fields. You can also see the Azure services and their sizing part of the solutions:

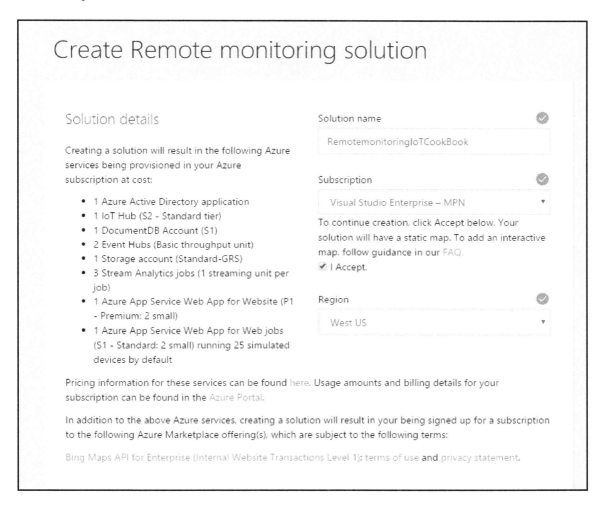

3. Azure IoT Suite will take a few minutes to configure and set up the remote monitoring solution:

Provision remote monitoring solution

4. Once the solution is ready, it will provide you the details and links to access it:

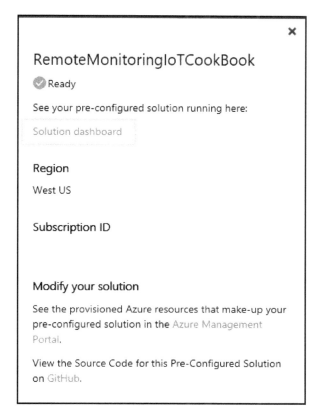

RemoteMonitoringIoTCookBook

✔ Ready

See your pre-configured solution running here:

Solution dashboard

Region

West US

Subscription ID

Modify your solution

See the provisioned Azure resources that make-up your pre-configured solution in the Azure Management Portal.

View the Source Code for this Pre-Configured Solution on GitHub.

Remote monitoring solution is ready

5. After your solution is ready, the next step is to navigate to the link for the dashboard.
6. Click on the **Sign in** button. This will authenticate the login credential which we just used to create the IoT Suite solution.
7. Accept the user authentication once you are prompted to.

8. You will land on the dashboard screen with the simulator device already ingesting the sample data to the IoT Hub:

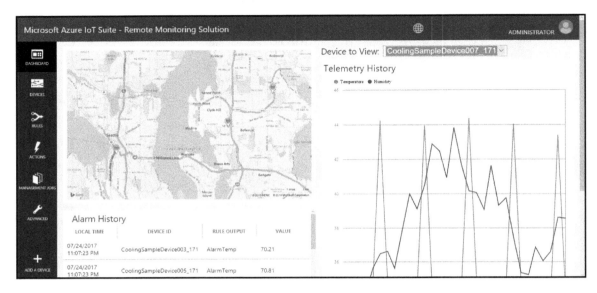

Dashboard screen for remote monitoring

9. The device menu shows all the list of devices with their current status, firmware version, and so on, all these are simulated devices connected to this IoT solution:

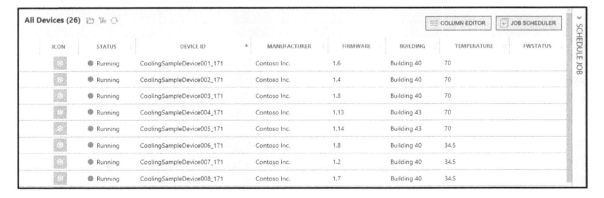

Device listing

10. Click on the **JOB SCHEDULER** in the top right corner to create a job for the selected device and update the device twin information for all devices:

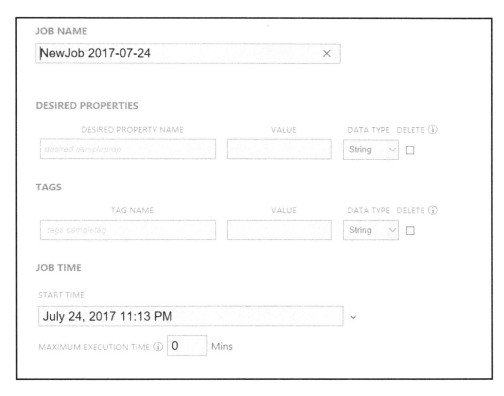

Device twin update job

11. The other two operations that we can perform are: edit the device icon and invoke a direct method on the scheduled date and time.

12. To update individual device details, select any device from the list:

> DEVICE DETAILS

Disable Device

Add Rule...

Commands

Methods

Device Twin ⓘ   Download

> Tags   Edit
> Desired Properties   Edit
> Reported Properties

> Device Properties
˅ Recent Jobs

    No Jobs

View selected device details

13. Navigate to the **Rules** menu for the list of alarms created for various devices:

Rules (50)

STATUS	RULE ID	DEVICE ID	DATA FIELD	OPERATOR	THRESHOLD	RULE OUTPUT
⬤ Enabled	65c510a7-4a40-489c-8cc3-40a14cdbdacd	CoolingSampleDevice001_171	Temperature	>	60.00	AlarmTemp
⬤ Enabled	f43700f9-25b3-44e0-9873-28718d9e2d21	CoolingSampleDevice001_171	Humidity	>	48.00	AlarmHumidity
⬤ Enabled	9333fb9c-2d0a-47d0-aa41-4e14b7616880	CoolingSampleDevice002_171	Temperature	>	60.00	AlarmTemp
⬤ Enabled	da72c646-0501-4c61-8f72-368a2e4718b8	CoolingSampleDevice002_171	Humidity	>	48.00	AlarmHumidity
⬤ Enabled	173a00fa-96f0-437e-9ad5-466116295b3b	CoolingSampleDevice003_171	Humidity	>	48.00	AlarmHumidity
⬤ Enabled	22c83302-3635-43e5-acb6-2850e821bb31	CoolingSampleDevice003_171	Temperature	>	60.00	AlarmTemp
⬤ Enabled	75ba2a75-c4e4-402f-b55c-90571dd2049c	CoolingSampleDevice004_171	Temperature	>	60.00	AlarmTemp
⬤ Enabled	c403a2fd-1b6e-4d85-adab-074c4a176941	CoolingSampleDevice004_171	Humidity	>	48.00	AlarmHumidity

List of all existing alarms

14. We can select any individual alarm to see the details, as shown in the following screenshot:

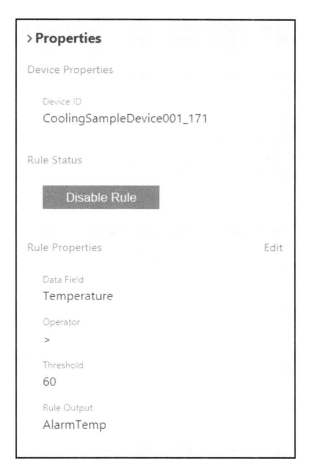

View selected alarm details

15. Click on the **Add A Device** menu. You will get two options, as shown in the following screenshot:
    1. Add a new simulated device.
    2. Add a new custom device - a real device configured to connect with the IoT Hub of this solution.

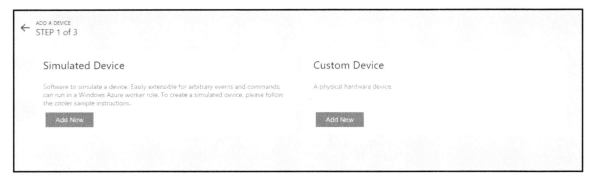

Add new device

How it works...

The solution once deployed in your Azure subscription, can be set to start the simulator device to send the telemetry data. Once the data infestation is started, the data flows through the stream analytics and the event hubs and gets processed and stored into the database.

The dashboard view shown as follows:

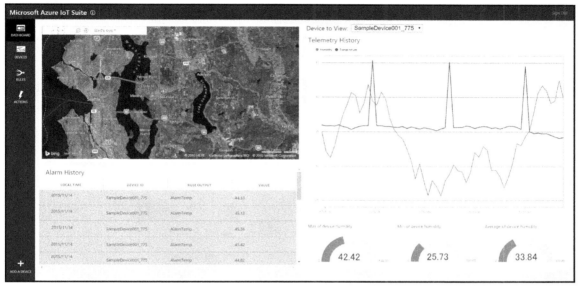

The devices section lists all the devices which are a part of this solution and can be managed. We can update their properties or statuses from this area. Another area rule defines the different thresholds based on which the **Azure Stream Analytics** (**ASA**) job acts and raises alarms.

There's more...

You can add your custom devices and connect to your remote monitoring solution. The **Add Device menu** on the portal navigation will guide you to your own custom devices.

We can connect a Raspberry Pi device to send the temperature and humidity sensor's data. Once the data has moved through the different components of the solution, it will be made available on the dashboard.

See also

You can delete the remote monitoring solution by navigating back to: Azureiotsuite.com.

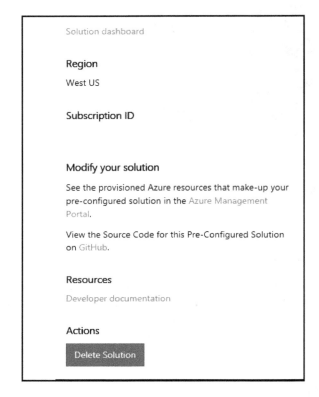

Delete existing solution

IoT Suite predictive maintenance

This predicts IoT device failures before they happen and systematically prevent them for millions of devices which are out in the fields. Using the real-time telemetry collection of data, a predictive model is created using Azure machine learning.

Getting ready

In predictive maintenance, the common scenario is focused on an asset failure and how it can be avoided using this solution. The example in this case is an airline engine being monitored, and based on its data, its predictive maintenance schedule is planned:

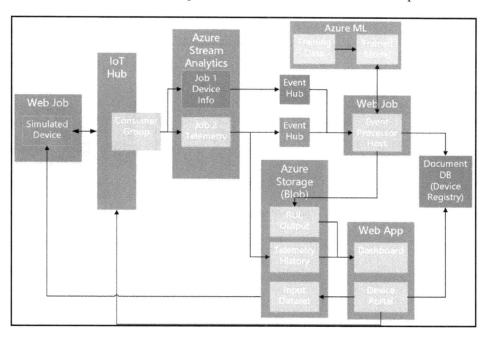

Predictive maintenance pre-configured solution architecture given by Azure

The Azure machine learning predefined model is used in this solution. The regression model is a publicly available template from the large gallery of prebuilt Azure ML models.

The model gets deployed into the Azure solution when we create the predictive maintenance solution.

How to do it...

In this section we will follow the following steps and will create the predictive maintenance solution:

1. To create a predictive maintenance solution, navigate to the site: `azureiotsuite.com`.

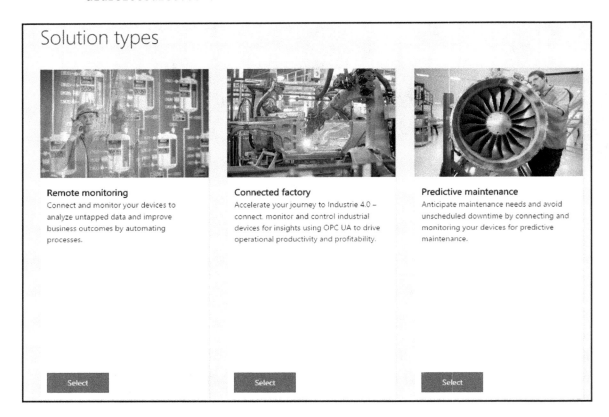

2. Provide the required fields. You can also see the Azure services and their sizing part of the solutions:

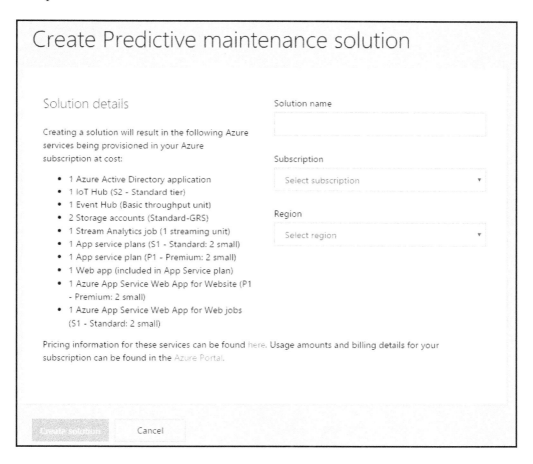

3. It will take a few minutes for the Azure IoT Suite to configure the predictive maintenance solution for you:

Provisioning predictive maintenance solution

4. Once the solution is created, you can click on **Solution dashboard** link to access dashboard:

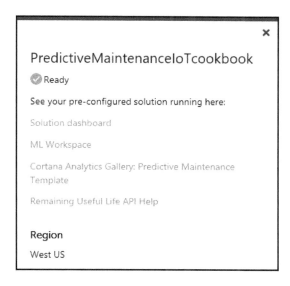

Predictive maintenance solution ready

5. On the dashboard you will see a button to start the simulator. This will start showing telemetry data on the dashboard:

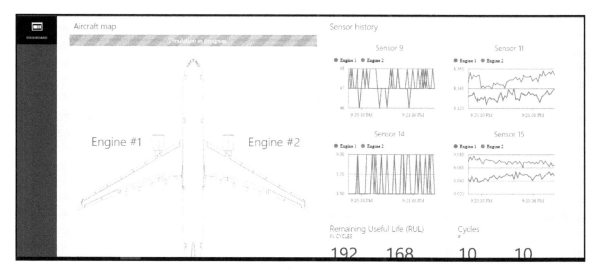

A dashboard for a predictive maintenance solution

6. You can see the output for the predictive analytics on the dashboard as shown in the following screenshot:

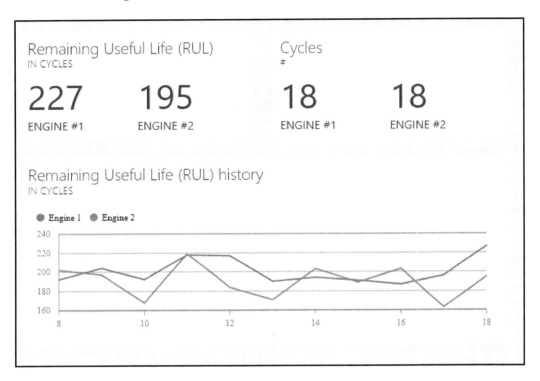

Prediction for remaining useful life

How it works...

The simulated aircraft engine device configured in the solution generates the required telemetry data. There are four different sensors devices transmitting data. This device also handles commands like StartTelemetry and StopTelemetry.

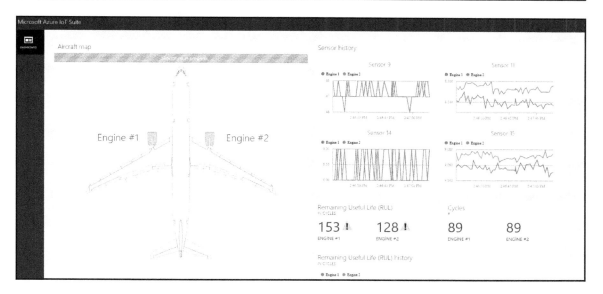

A predictive solution dashboard

The stream analytics job takes the responsibility to store the data into a Blob storage, which is later used to display the charts on the dashboard, as seen in the preceding diagram, and one output is consumed by the event processor host through the event hub.

The event processor host takes the sensors values and passes them to the API that exposes trained models to calculate the regression for an engine which is deployed in the Azure machine learning workspace.

You can navigate to `https://studio.azureml.net/` to view the model used for prediction.

There's more...

Azure IoT Suite predictive maintenance solution makes use of Azure machine learning to predict the remaining useful life of the sensor. It uses the sensor's telemetry data to train the algorithm and then make use of it. Using a web service the algorithm takes the input and can provide an output which is as shown on the dashboard.

The following screenshot shows the Azure machine learning algorithm used in this predictive maintenance solution:

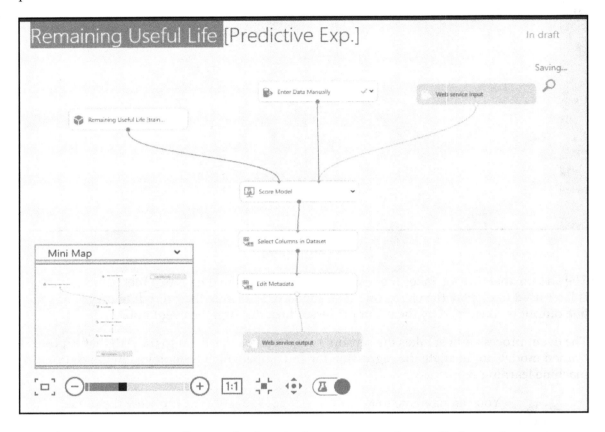

This algorithm automatically gets deployed when we create the predictive maintenance solution.

See also

You can delete the predictive maintenance solution by navigating back to:
`Azureiotsuite.com`.

Modify your solution

See the provisioned Azure resources that make-up your pre-configured solution in the Azure Management Portal.

View the Source Code for this Pre-Configured Solution on GitHub.

Resources

Developer documentation

Actions

Delete Solution

This will delete all the services as well as the Azure machine learning algorithm which was created for this predictive maintenance solution.

IoT Suite connected factory

The connected factory pre-configured solution shows the common industrial scenarios by connecting and monitoring the industrial devices. The solution features multiple connected factories across many locations in the world. It monitors the factory, production lines, stations, and so on, by collecting their data and controlling them remotely.

Getting ready

Once the solution is provisioned, we can navigate to the dashboard. This solution has different factories simulation implemented. It shows their location on the map view. The following charts show the overall equipment efficiency and some key performance indicator statuses and alerts:

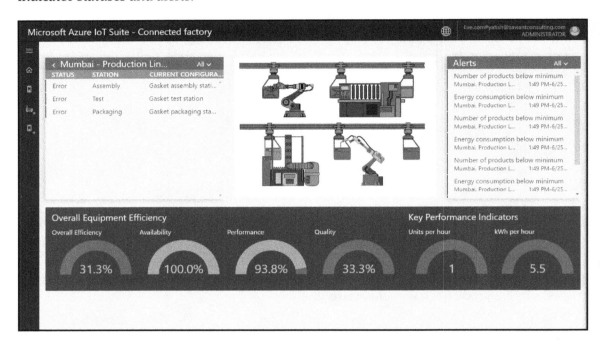

The factories panel allows us to select and drill down to any location and see the performance of the factory. It lists the status and configuration for the production line that we can select from.

The right panel shows the alerts based on the telemetry data. If an error occurs, it gets highlighted in this section:

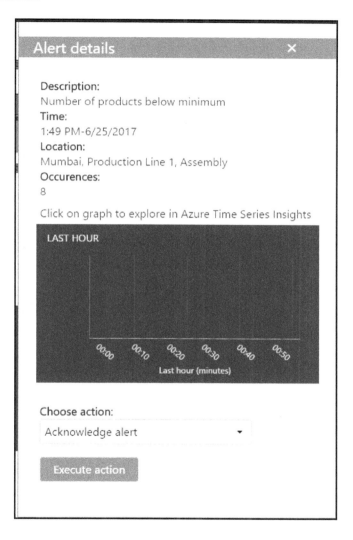

We can even filter these for a quick look up for the cause of failures:

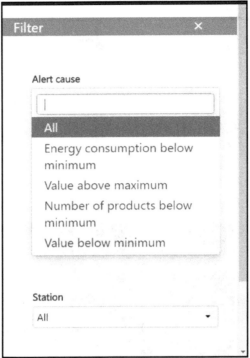

This solution also makes use of the newly released Azure Time Series Insights based on the alert data in a new environment of the service. As Microsoft states, *The Azure Time Series Insights, a fully managed analytics, storage, and visualization service that makes it incredibly simple to interactively and instantly explore and analyse billions of events.*

The bottom section shows the overall efficiency by using the operational parameters for factory processes. Overall efficiency is an industry standard which is calculated based on the availability rate, the performance rate, and the quality rate.

The following overall efficiency will be calculate as:

"OEE = availability x performance x quality"

How to do it...

In this section, we will create a pre-configured solution `Connected factory`:

1. To create a connected factory solution, navigate to the site: `azureiotsuite.com`.

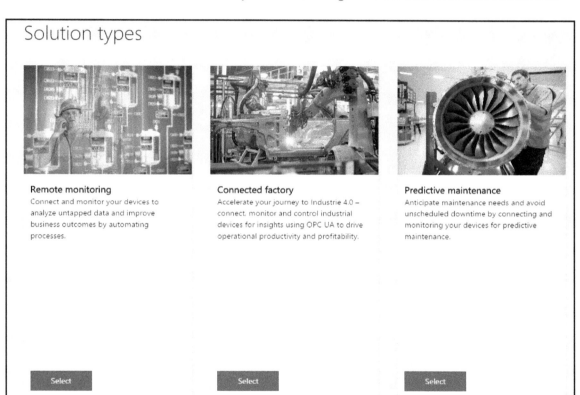

Solution types

Remote monitoring
Connect and monitor your devices to analyze untapped data and improve business outcomes by automating processes.

Connected factory
Accelerate your journey to Industrie 4.0 – connect, monitor and control industrial devices for insights using OPC UA to drive operational productivity and profitability.

Predictive maintenance
Anticipate maintenance needs and avoid unscheduled downtime by connecting and monitoring your devices for predictive maintenance.

Select

Select

Select

2. Provide the required fields. You can also see the Azure service and their sizing part of the solutions:

3. Once the solution is created, you can navigate to the link for the dashboard.

How it works...

The solution contains the simulated stations and the simulated **manufacturing execution system** (**MES**) to show the factory production line simulation. Microsoft has provided these simulated devices based on the **OPC Unified Architecture** (**OPC UA**) .NET standard that is published by the OPC Foundation. Azure has used the IoT edge for the OPC proxy and OPC publisher implementation:

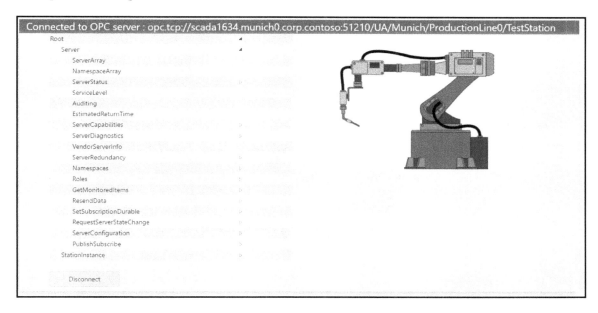

Connected factory - sensor configuration

IoT Hub is the source for Time Series Insights, which stores the data for up to 30 days as per the timestamp of the messages ingested into the hub. Currently, the Azure **Time Series Insights** (**TSI**) is in the preview mode. The time series view of node data comes directly from TSI using an aggregation for time span.

The web application deployed in the pre-configured solution is also an integrated OPC UA client. This solution also contains alerts processing, command and control, and visualization on the dashboard.

Customizing an IoT Suite

All the pre-configured solutions give us an end-to-end solution with complete integration of the multiple Azure Services as required to build an IoT solution. It does help in going live faster or doing a PoC with the nearest common scenarios we see based on each solutions capability.

But certainly, it may not be the exact solution you are looking for. You can extend and customize the solution for specific scenarios as you wish.

Let's understand how it works to customize the Remote monitoring pre-configured IoT Suite solutions.

How to do it...

In this recipe we will customize pre-configured solution:

1. Download remote monitoring: `https://www.github.com/Azure/azure-iot-rem ote-monitoring`.
2. Open the solution in Visual Studio.
3. Let's customize the telemetry data, that the simulator is sending.

How it works...

The code repository is well structured and it is easy to access the source code. To modify the telemetry message, navigate to `Simulator/Simulator.WebJob/Cooler/Telemetry/`.

The `RemoteMonitorTelemetry.cs` contains the `SendEventsAsync` method which forms the message body and then sends it further to get ingested into the IoT Hub.

We can add more parameters to this message body and can access those from stream analytics and process through the event processor host. The `RemoteMonitorTelemetryData` class contains the definition for the existing parameters being used for this telemetry data.

There's more

In this recipe we have done the Customisation for the remote monitoring pre-configured solution. similarly we can make custom changes to the other 2 pre-configured solution as well.

The customisation can be done at IoT hub where you can add message routing. one can modify the Stream analytics Jobs and their logic to process the telemetry data.

on the similar lines we can map our business operations with the pre-configured solution and make the necessary modifications.

Microsoft has made the source code open source. Their source code are available on GitHub for the IoT Suite pre-configured solution. The links for the these are as follows:

- Remote monitoring: `https://www.github.com/Azure/azure-iot-remote-monit oring`.
- Predictive maintenance: `https://github.com/Azure/azure-iot-predictive-m aintenance`.
- Connected factory: `https://github.com/Azure/azure-iot-connected-factory`.

7
Azure IoT Analytics

In this chapter, we will learn the following recipes:

- Connecting IoT Hub with Stream Analytics
- Real-time dashboard reports for IoT data using Power BI
- Azure Time Series Insights
- IoT Edge analytics using a simulator
- Real-time alerts with Azure functions

Introduction

Analytics are essential for the success of IoT solutions. It plays an important role in converting data into an intelligent action.

For any IoT solution, connecting a device and taking decisions are the core components and they are the main drivers for business transformations and digital business. IoT analytics solutions drives the business insight outcome. They help enhance and improve operational efficiency and asset performance by generating new revenue opportunities. With IoT implementation more business operation are getting automated. Because of which more data is getting generated, the data is of different variety and more complex.

IoT analytics provides a platform for data collection for Edge devices; it helps discover actionable insights. The Azure platform has the right tools and techniques at the right time to help an organization achieve business outcomes.

Azure IoT analytics has the capabilities of intelligent automation by using IoT platform integration with a combination of an advanced analytics data platform and machine learning. Gartner explained in the following image is about how business transforming with IoT Analytics, at link: `http://www.gartner.com/smarterwithgartner/transform-yo ur-business-with-iot-analytics/`.

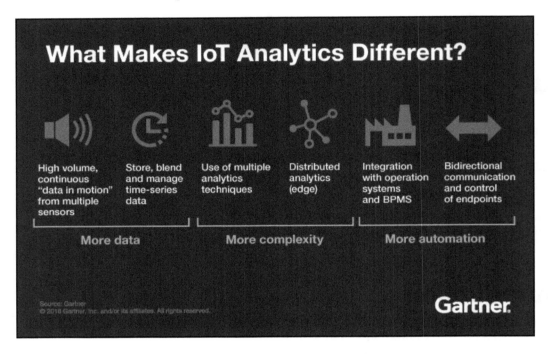

Gartner diagram showing how IoT analytics across Industries

Let's understand a few services with which we can connect with the IoT Hub and get required data from devices. We will be using this data to implement some analytics.

Understanding the Azure IoT lifecycle

This reference IoT lifecycle provides guidance for building secure and scalable, device-centric solutions for connecting devices, conducting analysis, and integration with backend systems using the Microsoft platform. While these solutions may be built on public, private, and hybrid Azure cloud components, the core guidance is focused on public cloud implementations. The concept of this IoT lifecycle is also generally applicable to any IoT solution implementations, at any scale.

IoT solution lifecycle

The reference IoT lifecycle aims to be neutral about any industries and use case scenarios and also neutral towards approaches for solutions and the behavior of devices. However, while the reference IoT lifecycle is abstract, the assumption is that realizations of the IoT solutions will be very concrete and aligned with industry standards or domain-specific design needs.

The reference IoT lifecycle provides flexibility for composability and extensibility to allow for a variety of technology choices driven by the specific solution requirements provided by the Microsoft Azure platform. The lifecycle also introduces foundational principles for the reference architecture, then presents the conceptual model and components of the IoT solution architecture, which can be implemented using the Azure platform:

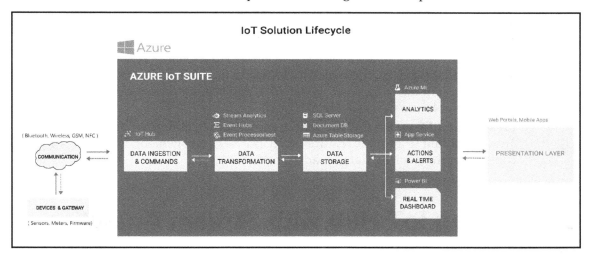

Azure IoT lifecycle designed by Saviant Consulting. www.SaviantConsulting.com

The preceding image shows the high-level conceptual IoT lifecycle. The Azure IoT lifecycle is composed of the Azure core platform services and the application-level components to facilitate end-to-end solution needs across three major areas of a typical IoT solution.

Components of the IoT solution lifecycle

You need to start by understanding the IoT lifecycle before you jump into the IoT solution.

This lifecycle talks about the stages of any IoT solution that it goes through, which are as follows:

- **Devices and gateway**: Identifies the IoT devices that will collect the data at their end and ingest it into the IoT Hub.
- **Communication**: This stage helps IoT devices to connect to the internet through GSM, Wi-Fi, Bluetooth, or any other networking techniques to connect to the internet.
- **Data ingestion**: Azure provides an IoT Hub to ingest data and manage devices and their messages.
- **Data transformation**: This stage transforms the data we receive from IoT devices into data that has to be processed.
- **Data storage**: You need to design storage strategies at this stage, transactional data sent by IoT devices and analytics needs to stored into databases.
- **Analytics, action and alert, and dashboard**: This stage gives alerts on insights into the IoT devices. It also defines preventive maintenance based on the data ingested by the device; these metrics will help us to take preventive measurement on the assets in the field. Also, a dashboard presentation can be done using Power BI tools.
- **Presentation layer**: Finally, the web or mobile applications are developed; these are suites build to provide features such as asset management, managing or controlling the devices, data, or advance analytics.

Connecting IoT Hub with Stream Analytics

Azure Stream Analytics provides the key capability of IoT solutions: real-time analytics on the data ingested. As Microsoft says, *Azure Stream Analytics is a fully managed service providing low latency, highly availability, and scalable complex event processing over streaming data in the cloud.*

Getting ready

Azure Streaming Analytics (**ASA**) accepts IoT Hub as the input for the Stream Analytics job. The output can be stored into the database or we can connect with Power BI to do the presentation.

Let's work in the next section to send sample data to the IoT Hub and connect with Stream Analytics.

How to do it...

Lets create a Stream Analytics service and connect with IoT Hub:

1. Create an IoT Hub in the Azure portal.
2. We will use the C#-based console application as a simulator to send the data.
3. Select **Stream Analytics job** from the **Internet of Things** menu:

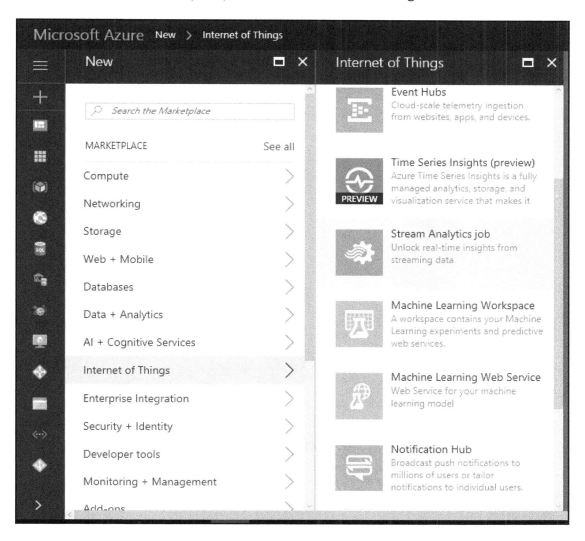

4. The next step is to create the Stream Analytics service:

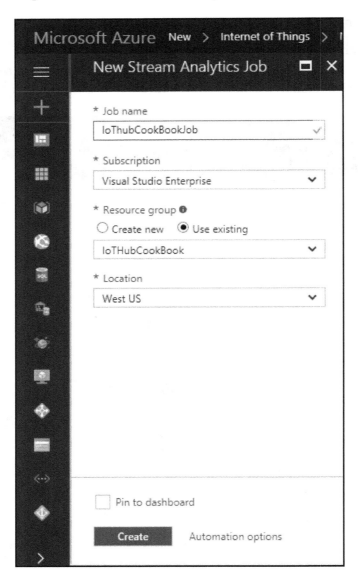

5. A job is created without any input or output configured:

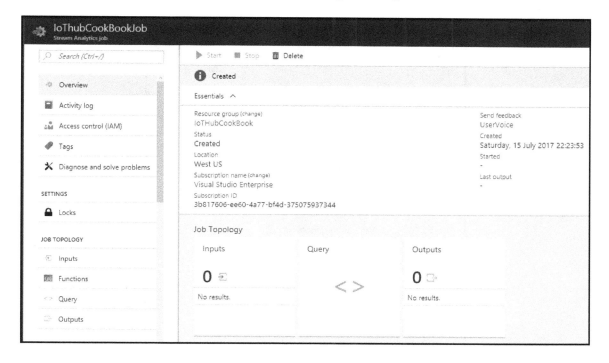

6. Select **Inputs** from the navigation to create an input:

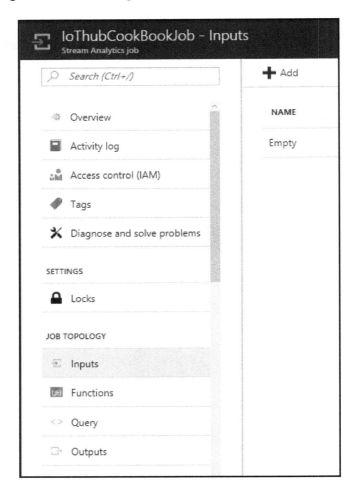

7. Provide details for creating a new job input with IoT Hub:

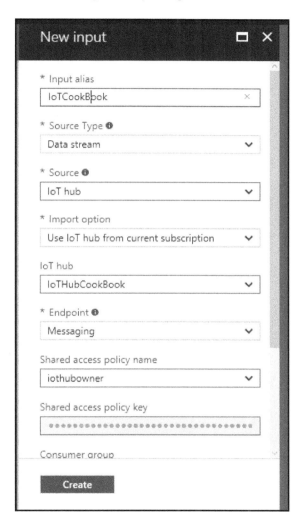

8. We can manage the job input created:

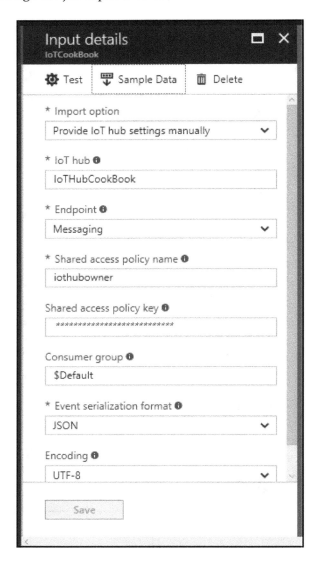

9. Create a job output for Stream Analytics:

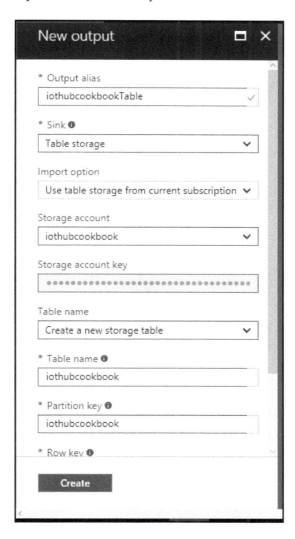

10. In the **Query** configuration, take the input from the IoT Hub input and provide it to the output:

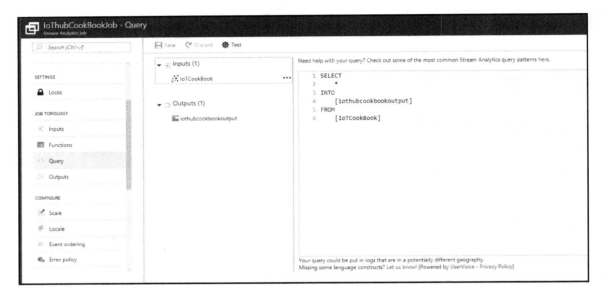

11. Stream Analytics Dashboard showing all details for newly created job and click **Start** at the top to initialize the job:

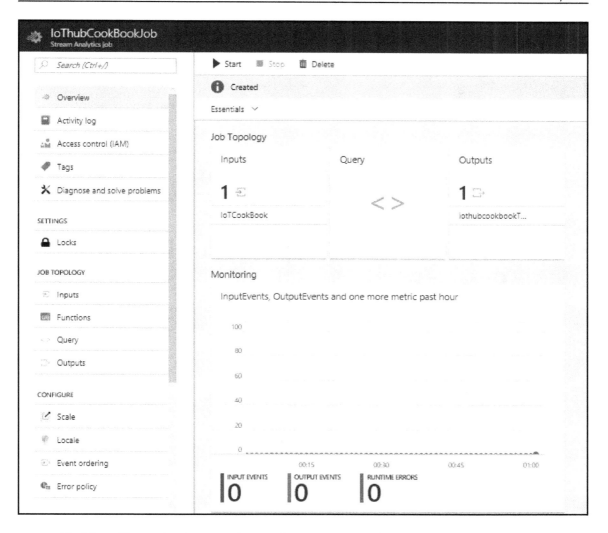

12. We will use the C# console simulator we created in `Chapter 3`, *IoT Hub Messaging and Commands*, it will send the telemetry data to IoT Hub.

13. We can see the output file created by the Stream Analytics job:

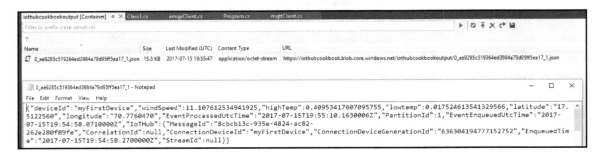

Real-time dashboard reports for IoT data using Power BI

An Azure Stream Analytics job provides various output methods; one of them is to directly provide data for Microsoft Power BI, a visualization tool that helps to take advantage of business intelligence with the most important metrics available at a glance.

Getting ready

We will continue to use the Azure subscription for the IoT Hub and Stream Analytics job; for Power BI we need to create an account. Navigate to the Power BI website, www.powerbi.com.

How to do it...

In this section, we will use the IoT Hub data to display in power BI:

1. Create an IoT Hub in the Azure portal.
2. We will use the C#-based console application as a simulator to send the data.
3. Navigate to the Power BI website, powerbi.com.
4. We will be using a default workspace.
5. We will use the Stream Analytics job that we created in the previous recipe.

6. Navigate to the output and create a new output for Power BI:

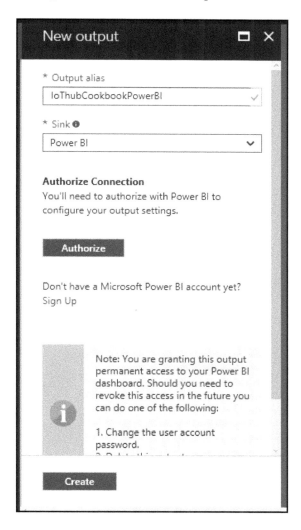

7. Authenticate the Power BI Account, so you can configure workspace details:

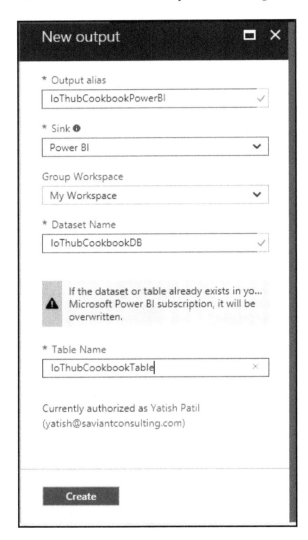

8. Save the details and create a new output:

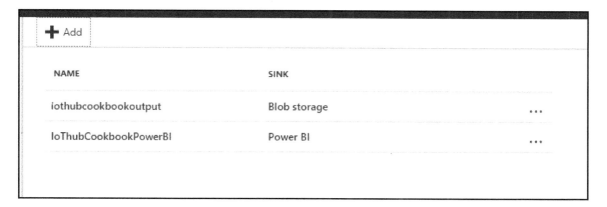

9. Modify the query to store data into the Power BI output:

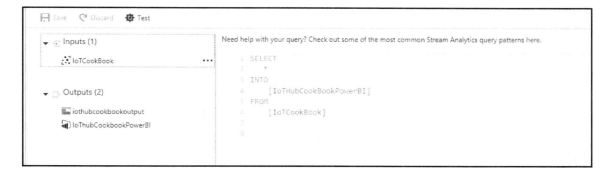

10. Run the IoT device simulator code, which will ingest new data into the IoT Hub:

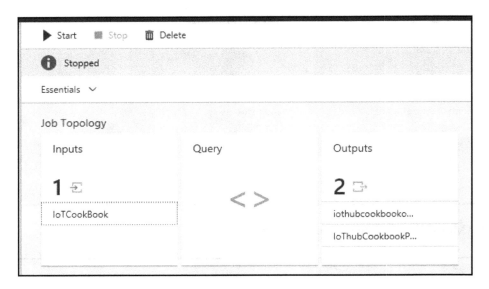

You will noticed here, we have created 2 output for our Stream Analytics job. This is the capability it provides. You can define 2 outputs depending on your solution need.

11. Navigate to the `PowerBi.com` and login so you can go to your workspace:

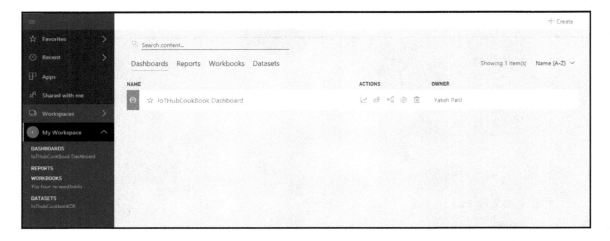

12. Under the **Datasets** tab, a new database will be created, which we configured in Stream Analytics job `IoTHubCookBookDB`:

13. From the **Action** button shown in preceding image, select **Create Report**:

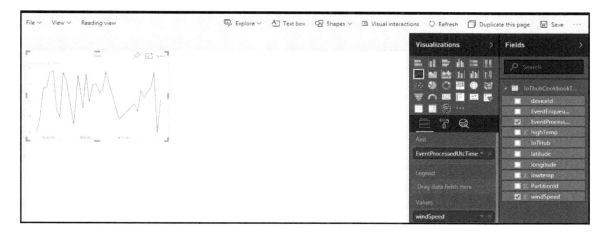

14. Complete the dashboard and save the report:

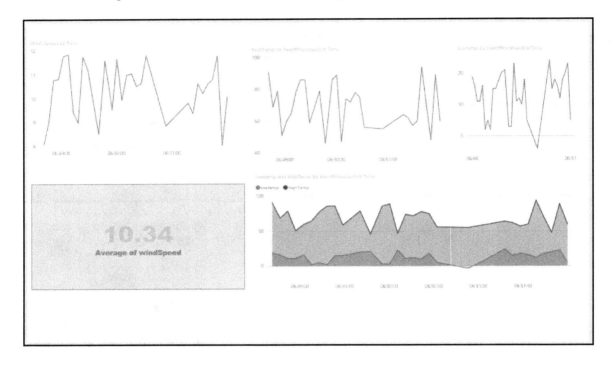

15. You can share the dashboard using different options as shown in the following screenshot:

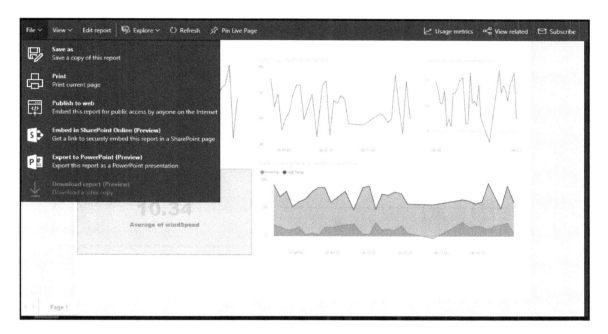

There's more...

You can learn more about Power BI dashboards, to create and share different visualization reports for your IoT solution. Follow the URL for more details on Power BI dashboards:

https://powerbi.microsoft.com/en-us/documentation/powerbi-service-dashboards/

Azure Time Series Insights

Time is the important factor in any IoT solution, as business outcomes are time-driven. The data that IoT solutions generate at every time interval just increases the huge data size. We need to implement a technology that can scale and provide analytics, and visualize it quickly.

Getting ready

As Microsoft says, *Azure Time Series Insights is a fully managed analytics, storage and visualization service that makes it simple to explore and analyze billions of IoT events simultaneously.* It helps you to quickly validate your IoT solution and avoid costly downtime to mission critical devices by helping you discover hidden trends, spot anomalies, and conduct root-cause analysis in near real-time.

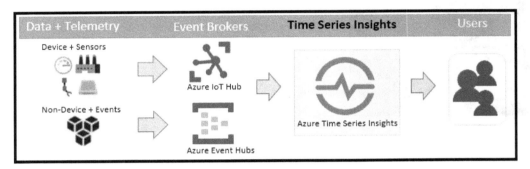

How Azure Time Series works

The key benefits that you get are as follows:

- It is easy to get started with; it does not require any data preparation
- In near real-time insights, it provides you with the output
- You can build custom solutions, and embed time series in existing applications
- Scalability is provided as with IoT Hub so it can perform the task in near real-time

How to do it...

We will create a Azure Time Series and will connect IoT Hub:

1. We will continue to use the IoT Hub `IoTHubCookBook`, we have created.
2. Select **Time Series Insights (preview)** from New – **Internet of Things**:

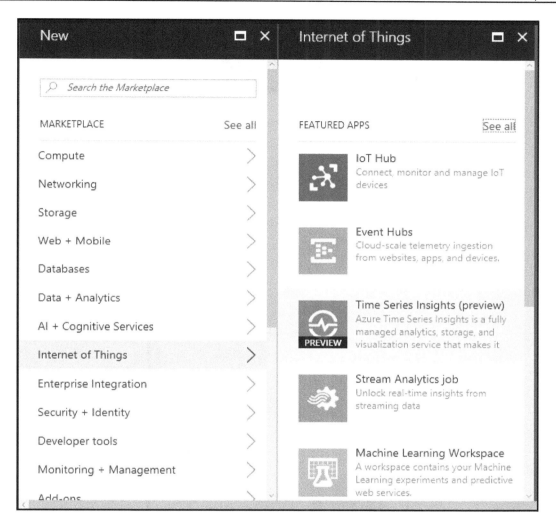

3. Create a new Time Series Insights called `TimeSeriesCookbook`:

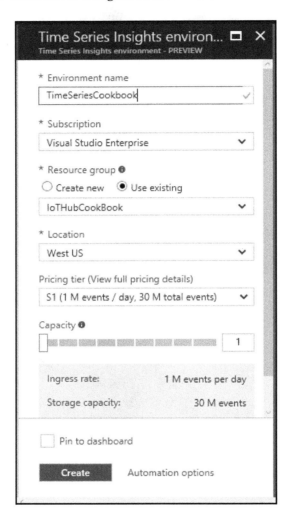

4. Once it is created, navigate to the dashboard:

5. Click on **Event** and hit **Add** to configure IoT Hub as the source:

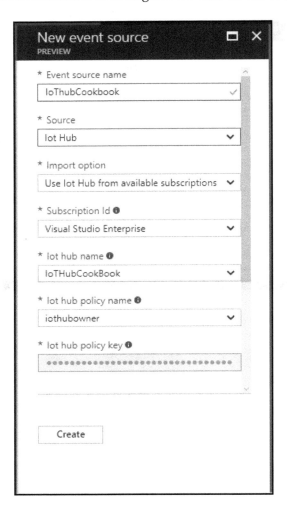

6. We need to define data access policy. You can add yourself or other users and provide the right access to them:

7. Click on **Go to Environment** to access Time Series Insights on the data you ingested to the IoT Hub:

8. View Azure Time Series Environment for real-time insights.

IoT Edge analytics using a simulator

Edge computing is the next stage for IoT solutions, with Microsoft recently releasing a new service for running analytics at Edge devices. Azure IoT platform is extending the capabilities; this service is called **IoT Edge**.

The new platform can run on Windows and Linux OS. It can run on devices with 128 MB memory. It provides modules to run Azure services like Azure functions, Stream Analytics, Azure's machine learning, and artificial intelligence capabilities which will all be available on IoT Edge.

As Microsoft Azure states, some of the benefits and advantages of using Azure IoT Edge are as follows:

- Perform edge analytics
- Deploy IoT solutions from cloud to edge
- Manage devices centrally from the cloud
- Enable real-time decisions
- Connect new and legacy devices
- Reduce bandwidth costs

Getting ready

In this recipe, we will be using an IoT Edge repository and a sample provided for ingesting messages: a device-to-cloud message. We will be using the device explorer to read the data we ingested.

The prerequisite requires on a local machine for working with IoT Edge are as follows:

1. Visual studio 2015 installed.
2. Git repository.
3. CMake.

How to do it...

In this section we will use the IoT Edge SDK and the simulator provided by it:

1. We will continue to use the IoT Hub `IoTHubCookBook` we created.
2. Clone the repository for IoT Edge to the local drive using a git command:

```
git clone https://github.com/Azure/iot-edge.git
```

3. Open the VS Command Prompt.
4. Navigate to the IoT Edge local repository folder.
5. Run the build command, which will compile and build the code to connect to the IoT Hub and run data ingestion:

```
tools\build.cmd --disable-native-remote-modules
```

6. It will take 20+ minutes to perform the task:

7. Once the build is completed, navigate to the samples
   \simulated_device_cloud_upload\src folder.
8. Edit the simulated_device_cloud_upload_win.json configuration file in
   Notepad.
9. We will configure the IoT Hub and device details in the sample module:

```
    },
    "args": {
      "IoTHubName": "IoTHubCookBook",
      "IoTHubSuffix": "azure-devices.net",
      "Transport": "HTTP"
    }
  },
  {
    "name": "mapping",
    "loader": {
      "name": "native",
      "entrypoint": {
        "module.path": "..\\..\\..\\modules\\identitymap\\Debug\\identity_map.dll"
      }
    },
    "args": [
      {
        "macAddress": "01:01:01:01:01:01",
        "deviceId": "myFirstDevice",
        "deviceKey": "LKCXsBKMKISTjr3ii08UXgIpELxy8/38EiMuxNAiqek=",
      },
```

10. To run this simulator we will execute the following code:

```
samples\simulated_device_cloud_upload\Debug\simulated_device_cloud_
upload_sample.exe
..\samples\simulated_device_cloud_upload\src\simulated_device_cloud
_upload_win.json
```

11. The simulator will start and data will get ingested:

12. Open the device explorer and monitor the readings:

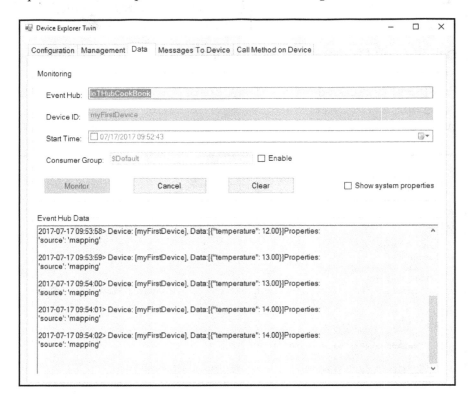

Real-time alerts with Azure functions

Azure functions are small running pieces of code, or functions, in the cloud. You can write small pieces of code that you need for a specific problem without worrying about the complete application or the infrastructure where we can run it.

There are various existing connectivity options available along with language support.

We will be exposing communication with IoT Hub and exploring how Azure functions can work with our small piece of code.

How to do it...

We will create a Azure function and see how to access IoT Hub real time:

1. We will continue to use the IoT Hub `IoTHubCookBook` we created earlier.
2. Select the Azure function app from new – compute:

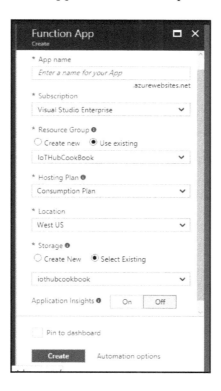

3. Create a new function app, FNCookBook:

4. Navigate to the function list view, and click the + icon to add a new function.
5. Azure function provides multiple templates; we will be selecting the language as C# and the scenario as Data Processing:

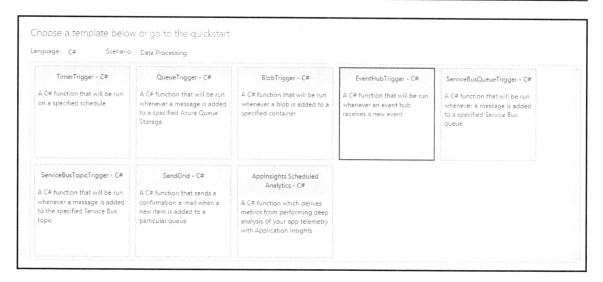

6. As shown in the following image, input the function name, and select the IoT
   Hub from the drop-down for binding:

7. Once you have created your app, the dashboard will look like this:

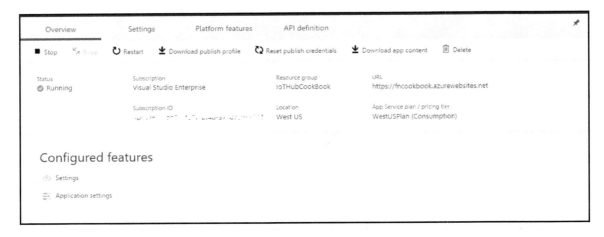

8. Select the function you created and it will navigate you to it:

9. On the right side, view the project files:

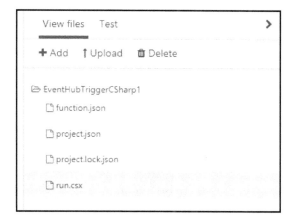

10. Define the project dependency and add the NuGet package declaration:

```
project.json    Save          ▶ Run
 1  {
 2    "frameworks": {
 3      "net46": {
 4        "dependencies": {
 5          "Microsoft.AspNet.WebApi.Client": "5.2.3",
 6          "Microsoft.AspNet.WebApi.Core": "5.2.3",
 7          "Microsoft.Azure.Amqp": "1.1.5",
 8          "Microsoft.Azure.Devices": "1.0.9",
 9          "Newtonsoft.Json": "8.0.3"
10        }
11      }
12    }
13  }
```

11. We will write a code to read the message, parse it, and log it to the console:

```
run.csx        Save          ▶ Run

 1  using System;
 2  using Newtonsoft.Json;
 3  using Microsoft.Azure.Devices;
 4  using System.Text;
 5
 6
 7  class IoTHubDevicetoCloud {
 8      public string deviceid { get; set;}
 9      public DateTime timestamp {get; set;}
10      public float windSpeed {get; set;}
11  }
12
13  public static void Run(string myEventHubMessage, TraceWriter log)
14  {
15      log.Info($"C# Event Hub trigger function processed a message: {myEventHubMe
16
17
18      IoTHubDevicetoCloud eventHubMessage = JsonConvert.DeserializeObject<IoTHub
19
20          //More log messages, just helps you debug this function in the portal
21          log.Info($"deviceid: {eventHubMessage.deviceid}");
22          log.Info($"timestamp: {eventHubMessage.timestamp}");
23          log.Info($"temperature: {eventHubMessage.windSpeed}");
24  }
25
```

12. The logs window will show the output:

```
Logs                                    ▮▮ Pause  ▤ Clear  ▢ Copy logs  ⤢ Expand  ⌄

2017-07-19T18:25:10  No new trace in the past 2 min(s).
2017-07-19T18:26:00.593 Function started (Id=9d1ab090-7f10-456e-9dc8-c59156be126c)
2017-07-19T18:26:00.843 C# Event Hub trigger function processed a message: {"deviceId":"myFirstD
2017-07-19T18:26:00.843 deviceid: myFirstDevice
2017-07-19T18:26:00.843 timestamp: 1/1/0001 12:00:00 AM
2017-07-19T18:26:00.843 temperature: 9.217585
2017-07-19T18:26:00.843 Function completed (Success, Id=9d1ab090-7f10-456e-9dc8-c59156be126c, Du
```

There's more...

The Azure function application has the advantage of being simple and flexible; it also provides a way to output triggers similar to the input trigger that we configured with IoT Hub.

Consider the scenario of raising a critical alarm once the temperature goes outside the permitted range. We can identify if the threshold is missed by the current temperature reading and we can send a command, cloud-to-device and back to the IoT Hub. We can even make use of custom endpoints and route the message to a new endpoint that a will have a different processing.

You can use the Microsoft Azure documentation to take function application to the next level, and build some interesting solutions using advance integrations of the IoT Hub.

8

Using Real Devices to Connect and Implement Azure IoT Hub

In this chapter, you will learn following recipes:

- Install Windows IoT Core on Raspberry Pi
- Connect and Configure IoT Core on Raspberry Pi
- Demo - smart parking
- Demo - temperature and humidity
- Using an online Raspberry Pi simulator

Install Windows IoT Core on Raspberry Pi

In this recipe, we will be installing a Windows IoT Core on a Raspberry Pi 2 device. Windows 10 IoT Core is a version of Windows 10 for the IoT device. We can develop a **Universal Windows Platform (UWP)** app using the Visual Studio and install them on Raspberry Pi. This device can act as a gateway or end device depending on the implementation we plan.

Getting ready

You will require the IoT Core dashboard tool that provisions Windows 10 IoT Core and manages devices.

You can download it from here: `http://go.microsoft.com/fwlink/?LinkID=708576`.

How to do it...

This recipe, will set the Windows IoT Core upon the Raspberry Pi device:

1. Download and install the IoT dashboard.
2. Select **Set up a new device**:

Set up a new device

3. Connect the SD card via the memory card reader.
4. The default name for the device will be **minwinpc**.
5. You will need to provide the default password, which will be used while managing or connecting the device through the network.

There's more...

The Windows IoT Core project templates enable development for Windows IoT Core devices (such as Raspberry Pi 2 and 3, Minnowboard Max, and DragonBoard 410c) using Visual Studio 2015.

You can download and install the extension from `https://marketplace.visualstudio.com/items?itemName=MicrosoftIoT.WindowsIoTCoreProjectTemplates`.

Once you install this extension, you can create a new project Visual Studio for creating apps that run on the Raspberry Pi device based on UWP, C# development:

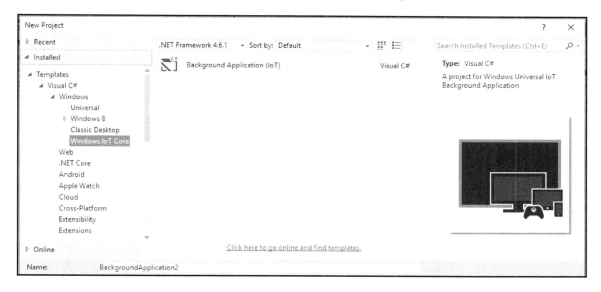

Create a new project

Connect and configure IoT Core on Raspberry Pi

In this recipe, we will be connecting the Raspberry Pi with our local machine using a network cable. The tasks that we will be doing are to connect and manage the Raspberry Pi from our local machine.

Getting ready

You will require the installed version of IoT dashboard, a Raspberry Pi device with the newly installed Windows IoT Core SD card, from the previous recipe.

We will explore the different options Windows IoT Core provides for managing the Raspberry Pi device.

How to do it...

In this recipe, we will use the IoT dashboard tool to manage the Raspberry Pi:

1. Insert the Windows IoT Core installed SD card in Raspberry Pi 2.
2. Connect the power cable and network cable to the Raspberry Pi from the local machine.
3. Once the device is connected, you will see it listed on the **My devices** section of the IoT dashboard tool:

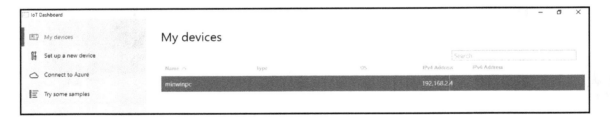

IoT dashboard for connected Raspberry PI

4. Once you right-click on the selected device, you will get the different options for you to manage:

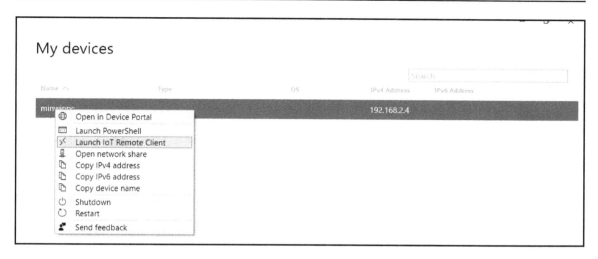

Connecting the IoT device

5. We will be selecting **Open in Device Portal**:

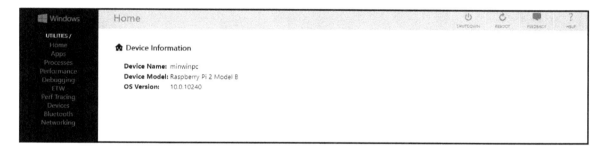

Dashboard for connected device in browser

6. Navigate to the **Apps** menu to see all the installed apps or install a new app on the Raspberry Pi.

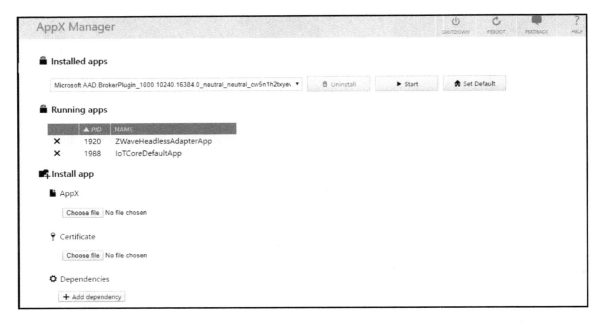

Manage apps for connected device

7. We will be creating a new app in the upcoming recipe and will be deploying it to the device.

8. Let's visit the **Networking** page to get the network details for the connected device:

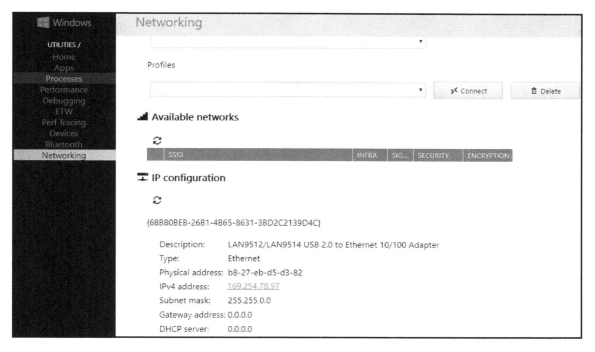

View network details

9. We can easily monitor the CPU, I/O, and memory usage using the **Performance** page:

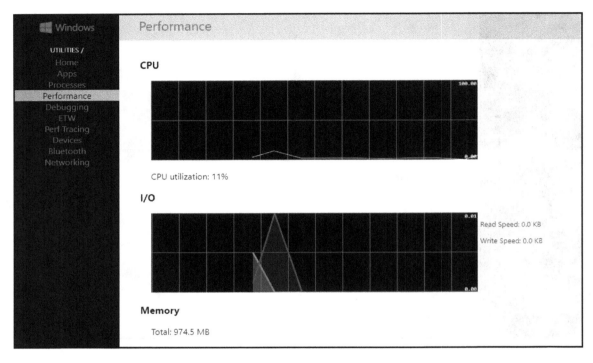

View performance metrics

There's more...

The following image shows the GPIO Pinout is design of the Raspberry Pi device:

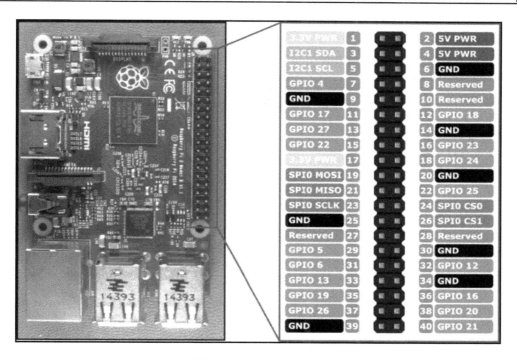

Raspberry Pi PinOut structure, reference from rspberrypi.org

To understand the pin structure for Raspberry Pi, follow this URL:

```
https://www.raspberrypi.org/documentation/usage/gpio/
```

Demo - smart parking

Smart parking implementation needs the use of low cost sensors, real-time data, and applications that allow users to monitor available and unavailable parking spots.

Using an IoT connected parking solution, we can help users to identify the open parking slot and navigate them to the right place. This will eventually have multiple benefits. Some of them are:

- Optimized parking
- Reduction in fuel consumption
- Managing traffic

Getting ready

We will use Raspberry Pi with Windows IoT Core installed on it. You can follow the recipe *Install Windows IoT Core on Raspberry Pi* from this chapter to install it.

The ultra sonic sensor that we will be using for this practical has the following four pins:

- VCC (V)
- GND (G)
- Echo
- Trigger

Voltage divider

The ECHO output is of 5v. The input pin of Raspberry Pi GPIO is rated at 3.3v. So to convert the 5v to the unprotected 3.3v input pin we use the voltage divider.

we use a voltage divider circuit using 1kΩ for R1 and a 2kΩ resistor to bring down the voltage to 3.3V.

Connecting Raspberry PI with sensors

- Connect the 5v (P2) to VCC (V) pin of Sensor
- GND (P6) into negative rail of the breadboard
- GPIO23 (P16) to Trigger
- GPIO24 (P18) into rail & link 1kΩ resistor
- Connect 1kΩ resistor with a rail connected with 1kΩ
- Link 2kΩ with Ground

How to do it...

In this recipe, we will follow the following steps to create parking sensors and send data to the IoT Hub:

1. Create a C# blank **Universal Windows Platform (UWP)** app from Visual Studio:

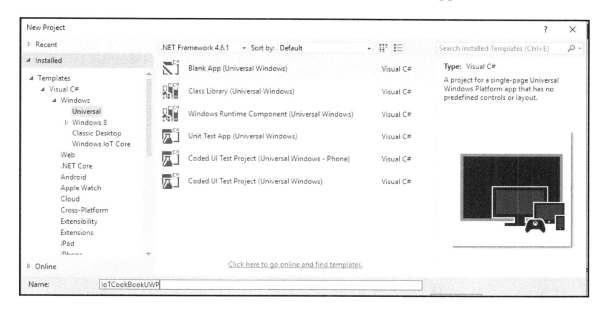

2. Add a reference for Windows IoT extension for UWP:

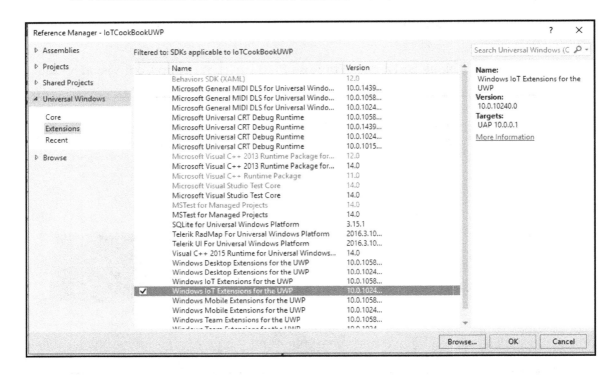

3. Add a NuGet package for **Microsoft.Azure.Devices.Client, Newtonsoft.JSON, Microsoft.Netcore.Universalwindowsplatform** packages as listed in the following screenshot:

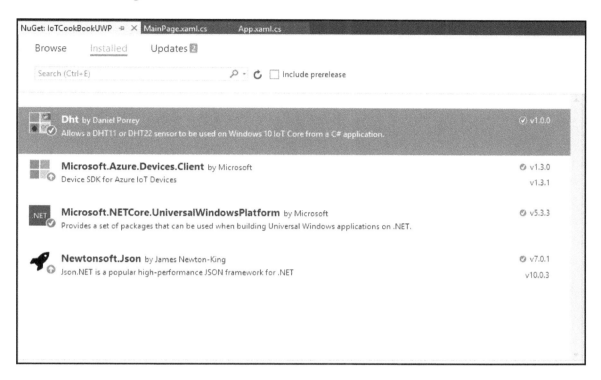

4. We will declare all devices and the IoT Hub and initialize them in the constructor:

```
const int intEchoPin = 23;
        const int intTriggerPin = 18;
        GpioPin pinEcho;
        GpioPin pinTrigger;
        DispatcherTimer timer;
        Stopwatch sw;
        static DeviceClient deviceClient;
        readonly string iotHubUri = "IoTHubCookBook.azure-
devices.net";
        readonly string deviceName = "myFirstDevice";
        readonly string deviceKey =
"LKCXsBKMKISTjr3ii08UXgIpELxy8/38EiMuxNAiqek=";
```

5. We should also initialize the `Gpio` pins of the Raspberry Pi devices that we defined in the *Getting ready* section:

```
var gpio = GpioController.GetDefault();
pinEcho = gpio.OpenPin(intEchoPin);
pinTrigger = gpio.OpenPin(intTriggerPin);
pinTrigger.SetDriveMode(GpioPinDriveMode.Output);
pinEcho.SetDriveMode(GpioPinDriveMode.Input);
pinTrigger.Write(GpioPinValue.Low);
```

6. We will create a timer tick event and define the interval to 60 seconds:

```
timer = new DispatcherTimer();
            timer.Interval = TimeSpan.FromSeconds(60);
            timer.Tick += Timer_Tick;
```

7. For every 60 seconds, we will measure the distance and send a cloud message containing the availability of the parking slot:

```
pinTrigger.Write(GpioPinValue.High);
            await Task.Delay(10);
            pinTrigger.Write(GpioPinValue.Low);
            sw.Start();
            while (pinEcho.Read() == GpioPinValue.Low)
            {
                // no implementation
            }
            while (pinEcho.Read() == GpioPinValue.High)
            {
                // no implementation
            }
            sw.Stop();

            var elapsed = sw.Elapsed.TotalSeconds;
            var distance = elapsed * 34000;
            distance /= 2;

            if (distance < 14)
            {
                // Send the parking availability status to Cloud
via Data integsation
                SendDeviceToCloudMessagesAsync(deviceName,
lastUpdated, false);
            }
            else
            {
                // Send the parking availability status to Cloud
```

```
via Data integsation
                SendDeviceToCloudMessagesAsync(deviceName,
lastUpdated, true);
            }
```

8. Depending on the data ingestion, we will write our parsing logic update and display it using a web or mobile app for the users.

How it works...

This demo is to show how a Raspberry Pi connected with a sensor is used to help implement a smart city solution. The device sends data for a parking slot and using a mobile or web interface, users can see the availability or navigation to the right place. Using some advance analytics, like predictive analytics, can help users to plan their visit.

The advantages of this solution are that it reduce the fuel consumption, creates a controlled traffic environment, and optimizes spaces for parking. It can be implemented at a university campus or offices, shopping centers, and so on.

Demo - temperature and humidity

In logistics/supply chain, a cold chain monitoring solution helps track the perishable products, eatables and food items are required to be delivered with some set temperature. The cold chain monitoring solution assures these will be delivered. This solution can have multiple analytics features build into it. With this solutions use of real-time analytics in combination of predictive analytics it will benefit the business.

Some of the benefits are:

- Increased productivity and supply chain efficiency
- Reduced operational costs
- Improved inventory accuracy

Getting ready

In this recipe, we will be using a DHT temperature and humidity sensor.

This sensor has 4 pins: VCC, Signal, unused, ground. The connection goes as follows:

- 3.3v (P1) -> VCC (V)
- GND (P6) -> GND (G)
- GPIO4 (P7) -> DATA (S)

How to do it...

In this recipe, we will use the temperature sensor to send data to the IoT Hub using Raspberry Pi:

1. Create a C# blank **Universal Windows Platform** (**UWP**) app from Visual Studio:

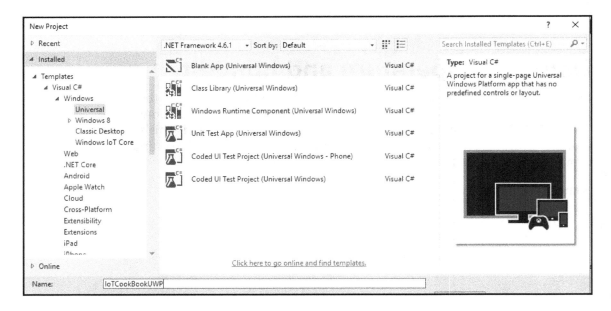

2. Add a reference for Windows IoT extension for the UWP:

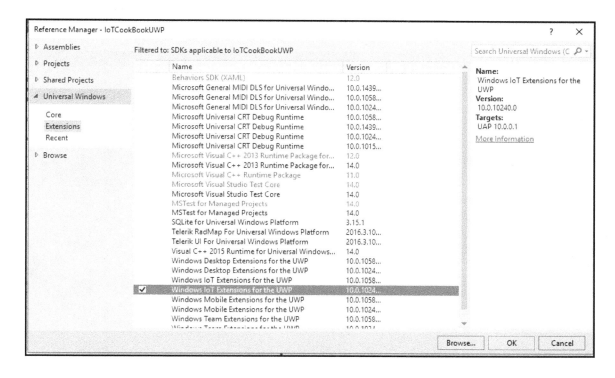

3. Add the NuGet packages for **Microsoft.Azure.Devices.Client, Newtonsoft.JSON, Microsoft.Netcore.Universalwindowsplatform** packages as shown in following screenshot:

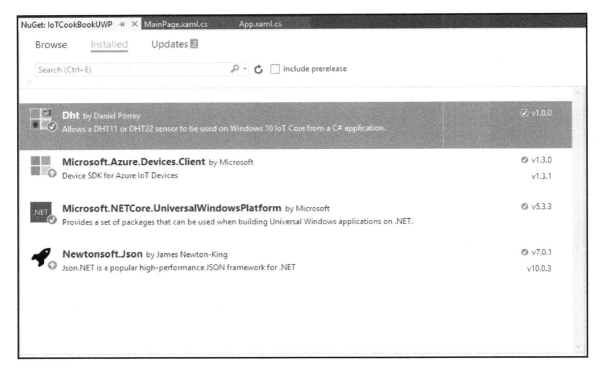

4. We will be using a C++ Universal library provided by Daniel Porrey.
5. Download the project `Sensors.Dht` from following link and include in your project:

```
https://github.com/porrey/dht/tree/master/source/Windows%2010%20I
oT%20Core/DHT%20Solution
```

6. Now we will add the reference of this `Sensors.Dht` project into our project `IoTCookBookUWP`:

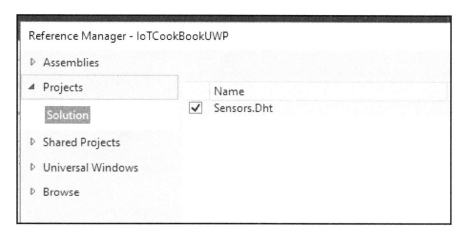

Add DHT reference to our UWP project

7. We will declare all the devices and the IoT Hub and initialize them in the constructor:

```
public DispatcherTimer _timer = new DispatcherTimer();
IDht _dht = null;
static DeviceClient deviceClient;
readonly string iotHubUri = "IoTHubCookBook.azure-devices.net";
readonly string deviceName = "myFirstDevice";
readonly string deviceKey =
"LKCXsBKMKISTjr3ii08UXgIpELxy8/38EiMuxNAiqek=";
```

8. We should also initialize the `Gpio` pins of the Raspberry Pi device, as we did in the *Getting ready* section:

```
_pin = GpioController.GetDefault().OpenPin(4,
GpioSharingMode.Exclusive);
_dht = new Dht11(_pin, GpioPinDriveMode.Input);
_timer.Interval = TimeSpan.FromSeconds(60);
_timer.Tick += _timer_Tick;
```

9. We will create a timer tick event and define the interval to 60 seconds:

```
timer = new DispatcherTimer();
timer.Interval = TimeSpan.FromSeconds(60);
timer.Tick += Timer_Tick;
```

10. For every 60 seconds, we will measure the distance and send a cloud message containing the availability of a parking slot:

```
try
{
DhtReading reading = new DhtReading();
float temperature = 0;
float humidity = 0;
DateTimeOffset lastUpdated;
if (reading.IsValid)
{
temperature = Convert.ToSingle(reading.Temperature);
humidity = Convert.ToSingle(reading.Humidity);
lastUpdated = DateTimeOffset.Now;
try
{
SendDeviceToCloudMessagesAsync(humidity.ToString(),
temperature.ToString(), lastUpdated, "");
}
catch (Exception ex)
{
// some code to handle exception
}
}
}
catch (Exception ex)
{
// some code to handle exception
}
```

11. Now ingest the data into the IoT Hub:

```
var telemetryDataPoint = new
 {
 deviceId = deviceName,
 time = DateTime.Now.ToString(),
 humidity = humidityDisplay,
 temperature = temperatureDisplay,
 LastReadTime = lastUpdated
 };
 var messageString =
JsonConvert.SerializeObject(telemetryDataPoint);
 var message = new Message(Encoding.ASCII.GetBytes(messageString));
 await deviceClient.SendEventAsync(message);
```

12. Depending on the data ingestion, we will write our parsing logic update and display it using a web or mobile app for the users.

How it works...

This demo is to show how a Raspberry Pi 2 connected with the sensor sends the temperature and humidity data to the IoT Hub. As the business of cold storage needs to deliver items with a certain temperature. This IoT Solution can be build to send critical alerts; example of this business case is: as soon as the temperature goes outside the expected threshold, alerts will be send to business users informing some attention required and demanding to take actions.

The advantages of this solution are that it helps to reduce fuel consumption, and increase, end customer satisfaction. This solution can be used in Logistics, food, or supply chain industry solutions.

Using an online Raspberry Pi simulator

You can use this online simulator tool to learn the basics of the Raspberry Pi device and how it connects with the IoT Hub. It is very simple and easy to configure and consume.

In this recipe, you will learn how a Raspberry Pi device can be used for sending device-to-cloud messages to the IoT Hub.

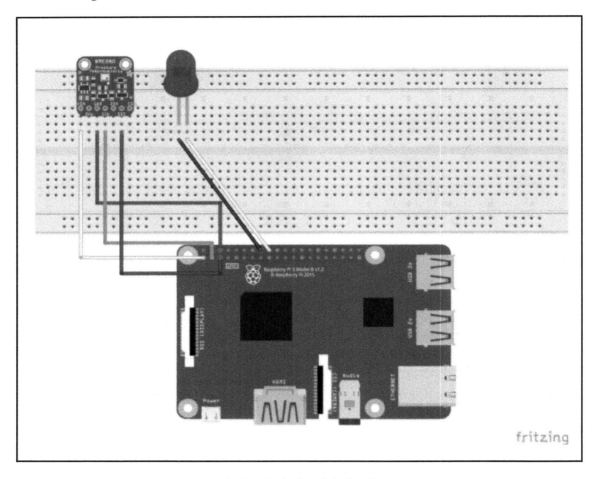

A web based simulator image for Raspberry Pi

How to do it...

Follow this recipe, to connect to an online simulator with the IoT Hub:

1. We will continue to use the IoT Hub `IoTHubCookBook` that we have created.
2. Open a new tab in the browser and use the link:

   ```
   https://azure-samples.github.io/raspberry-pi-web-simulator/
   ```

3. Get the device connection string from the device explorer.
4. Configure the simulator connection details for the device:

```
11    i2cBusNo: 1, // defaults to 1
12    i2cAddress: BME280.BME280_DEFAULT_I2C_ADDRESS() // defaults to 0x77
13  };
14
15  const connectionString = '[Your IoT hub device connection string]';
16  const LEDPin = 4;
17
18  var sendingMessage = false;
19  var messageId = 0;
20  var client, sensor;
21
22 ▾ function getMessage(cb) {
23    messageId++;
24    sensor.readSensorData()
25 ▾    .then(function (data) {
26 ▾      cb(JSON.stringify({
27          messageId: messageId,
28          deviceId: 'Raspberry Pi Web Client',
29          temperature: data.temperature_C,
30          humidity: data.humidity
31        }), data.temperature_C > 30);
32      })
33 ▾  ◂
```

Connecting with IoT Hub

5. Hit the **Run** button to start the simulated data ingestion:

```
Stop    Reset                                                                          ⌄
Sending message: {"messageId":2,"deviceId":"myFirstDevice","temperature":26.8614332244I821,"humid:
>
Message sent to Azure IoT Hub
>
Sending message: {"messageId":3,"deviceId":"myFirstDevice","temperature":23.711677246747836,"humid
>
Message sent to Azure IoT Hub
>
Sending message: {"messageId":4,"deviceId":"myFirstDevice","temperature":26.381356864545097,"humid
>
Message sent to Azure IoT Hub
> []
```

Web simulator sending data to IoT Hub

6. You can see the result using the device explorer by monitoring the device in **Data** tab. The output for the data being sent to the IoT Hub.

9
Managing the Azure IoT Hub

In this chapter, we will cover the following recipes:

- Device explorer for the Azure IoT Hub
- Using the IoT Hub command-line tool
- IoT Hub operation monitoring
- The diagnostic metrics of the Azure IoT Hub
- Scaling your IoT Hub solution

Introduction

In this book, we have learned how we can use the IoT Hub to connect, monitor, and control billions of Internet of Things assets. The Microsoft Azure IoT provides some tools that helps us to easily manage the IoT Hub services; these are open source tools.

In this chapter, we are going to look at a few ways on how we can manage the IoT Hub. The operation monitoring recipe will help you find out ways to debug your IoT Hub service and understand what is exactly happening in the service. At the end, we will look at ways to scale the IoT Hub instance.

Device explorer for the Azure IoT Hub

Microsoft Azure provides a tool device explorer, which helps you manage devices by connecting to the IoT Hub that you have created. It is simple to connect and perform some basic operations for device management, and it even reads messages, sends commands, and executes direct methods.

Getting ready

You can download the device explorer from `https://github.com/Azure/azure-iot-sdks/releases`. See the `SetupDeviceExplorer.msi` file available under the download section.

This tool gets installed on your local machine, and you can easily operate it. In this recipe, we are going to see how it is used for connecting and managing the IoT Hub. It works with IoT endpoints to perform the following task:

- Device identity management
- Receive device-to-cloud messages
- Send cloud-to-device messages

Using these, we can manage the devices in the IoT Hub, read device-to-cloud messages, and send cloud-to-device messages.

How to do it...

In this recipe, we will use the device explorer tool to manage the IoT Hub:

1. Download the device explorer from `https://github.com/Azure/azure-iot-sdks/releases`.
2. Install the tool at the default location `C:\Program Files (x86)\Microsoft\DeviceExplorer`.

3. Now run the `DeviceExplorer.exe` tool:

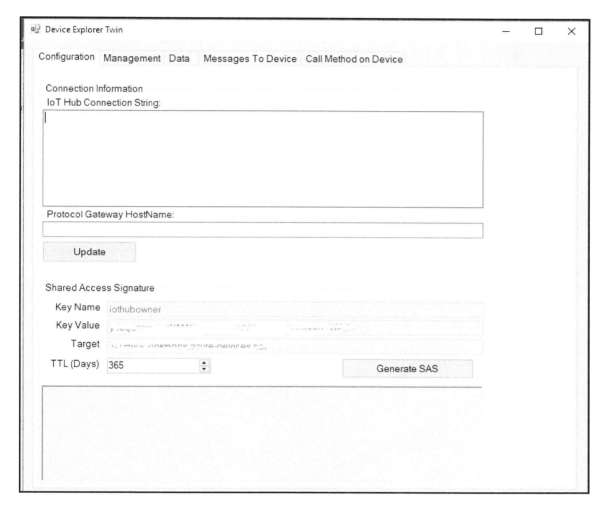

Device explorer connection with IoT Hub

4. From the Azure portal, navigate to the IoT Hub that you created, and copy the connection details for the IoT Hub owner access rights:

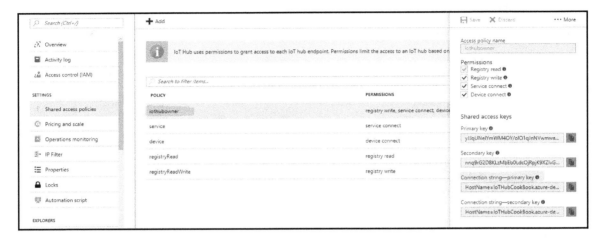

Connection string for IoT hub

5. In the device explorer tool, we will configure these details in the connection information and then hit the **Update** button:

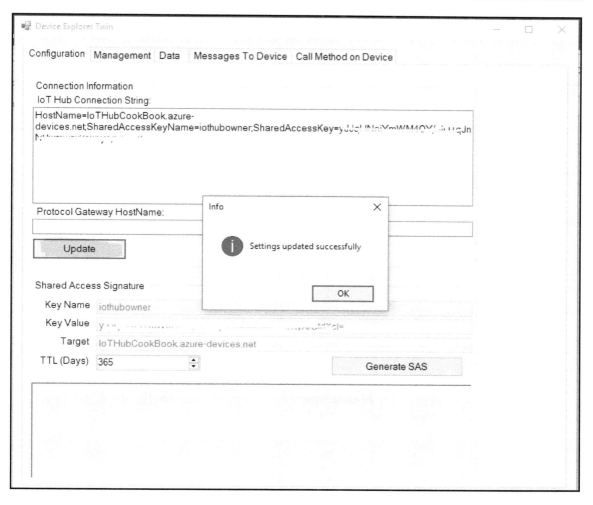

Connecting Device Explorer with IoT Hub

6. Once you are successfully connected with IoT Hub Service, you will be able to control the operations of device management and send or receive messages; and with the latest version, we can even call a direct method on the device:

Device explorer tabs

7. This tool also helps in creating the **Shared Access Signature**; we can use this in multiple scenarios. One of them is to connect an MQTT protocol directly with the IoT Hub:

Device explorer - Generate SAS Token

8. Now, let's move to the **Management** tab where we can see the list of existing devices that are connected to the IoT Hub:

Device explorer - list of devices

9. We can create a new device; you can provide the device ID for it:

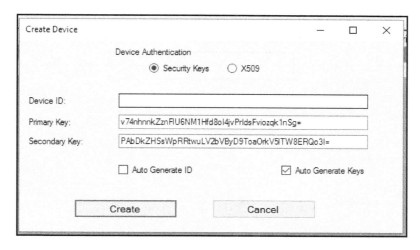

Device Explorer - Add New Device to IoT Hub

10. Once you have created a new device, you will need to know the device connection details, so you can configure it into the device itself:

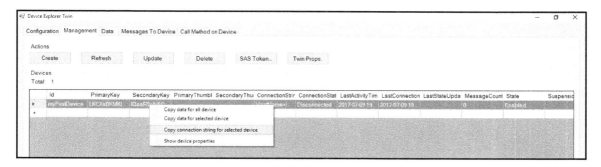

Device connection details

11. On right-clicking the selected device from the list, you will be able to get the required configuration details.

12. In `Chapter 2`, *Introducing Device Management,* about device twin. It is collection of properties specific to the individual device. The device twin is structured into 3 parts manly tags, **Desired Properties** and **Reported Propertie**s. We can click on the **Twin Props** to view these details from the device explorer tool:

Device twin information

13. We can use this **Data** tab, when a real device is connected and you would like to see the incoming messages before you implement your IoT solution, or when you want to debug for some purpose, you will be using the **Data** tab.

14. Navigate to the **Data** tab, select the device from the list, and hit the **Monitor** button:

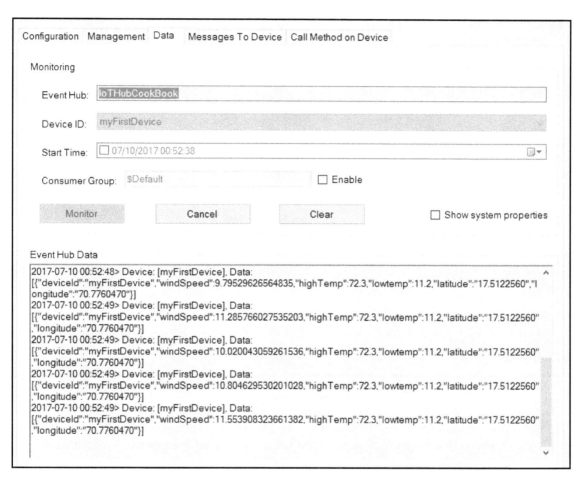

Device Explorer - View Device to Cloud Messages

15. After reading the device-to-cloud message, we can send a cloud-to-device message as well:

Device Explorer - Send Cloud to Device Message

16. You learned in `Chapter 2`, *Introducing Device Management,*that a direct method can be called on the IoT device; the latest version of the device explorer tool provides this option:

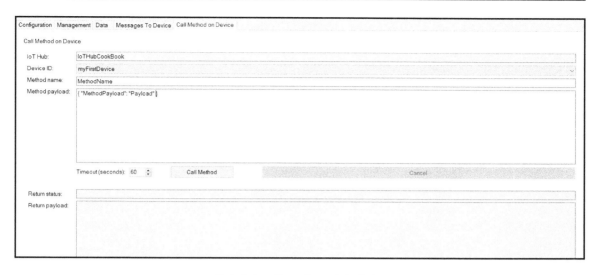

Device Explorer - Execute direct method on Device

Using the IoT Hub command-line tool

Azure IoT also provides a command-line tool called `iothub-explorer`. This tool helps you to manage the device registry from the hosted computer itself. It works for the following management options:

- Device twins
- Direct methods
- Cloud-to-device messages
- Device twin queries

This CLI tool is built using Node.js. In order to use the CLI command, we will need Node.js installed on the machine.

How to do it...

We will use the command-line tool, `iothub-explorer` in this recipe:

1. Install `iothub-explorer` tool by following the link: `https://github.com/azure/iothub-explorer`.

2. Connect to the IoT Hub using the connection string:

```
iothub-explorer login '<IoTHubConnectionString>
```

3. We will try and send a cloud-to-device message using this command:

```
iothub-explorer send myFirstDevice "Hello IoT Device"
```

There's more...

The cross-platform command-line tool is easy to install and is useful for quick troubleshooting or testing of your IoT device. When you run the `Help` command, it will list all the possible commands with the details and examples, for executing these commands in the CLI.

IoT Hub operation monitoring

Any business requires continuous monitoring of the operation to manage the risk and mitigate it by taking a proactive decision. Similarly, for any IoT solution, it is important to monitor the IoT Hub operations which include the devices communicating to the IoT Hub. The purpose is to improve their field operations, life span, performance, and to avoid any kind of risk occurring in field after device is deployed and increasing their effectiveness.

Getting ready

IoT solutions require monitoring at real-time, to find out the status of devices. IoT Hub provides an operation monitoring feature in Azure portal; this helps to track the device connectivity, device telemetry logs, data or file ingestion, and it also logs message routing events.

Events that IoT Hub monitors are as follows:

- Device identity operations
- Device telemetry
- Cloud-to-device messages
- Connections
- File uploads
- Message routing

How to do it...

In this section we will enable the **Operation monitoring**:

1. Log in to the Azure portal and navigate to the IoT Hub service.
2. Select the IoT Hub for which you want to enable the operation monitoring:

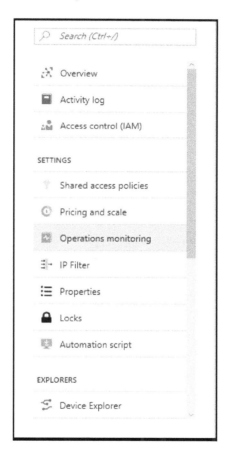

3. Select the events you would like to monitor:

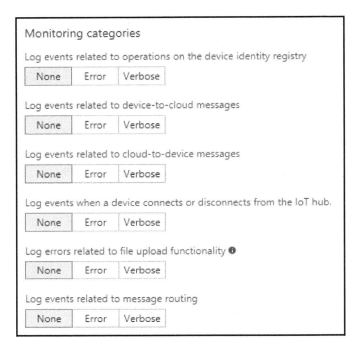

4. Save the selected configuration changes and the IoT Hub will start tracking the respective events:

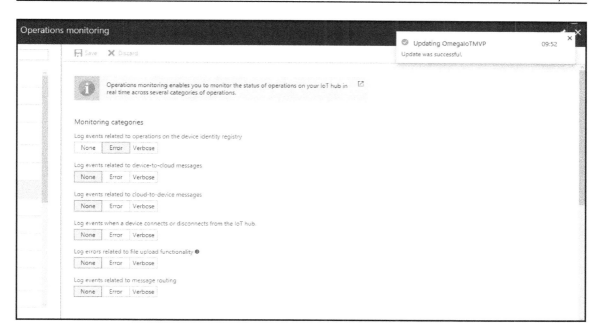

There's more...

Each monitoring operation tracks the following different types of events with the IoT Hub:

Device identity: This will be used to identify the errors with device creation, updates, or deletion from the IoT Hub identity registry.

Device telemetry: It will track errors related to the telemetry data sent by the IoT device to the IoT Hub; these errors can be seen in sending and receiving messages to and from the IoT device or the IoT Hub.

Cloud-to-device commands: We can use these to identify errors related to the IoT device communicating to cloud. When Cloud application sends any command to device using a cloud-to-device messages at the IoT Hub, such as errors in sending and receiving commands and receiving the command feedback.

Device connections: These will give a list of events; they will be the errors that occured when devices connect or disconnect with an IoT Hub. In these scenarios, a quick response to the device going offline may be crucial to avoid some business problems.

IoT Hub file uploads: When errors such as failed uploads or missing files occur, this will trigger an event indicating the failure, and users can plan an action based on this.

See also

Operation monitoring also exposes the event hub connectivity for these monitoring events:

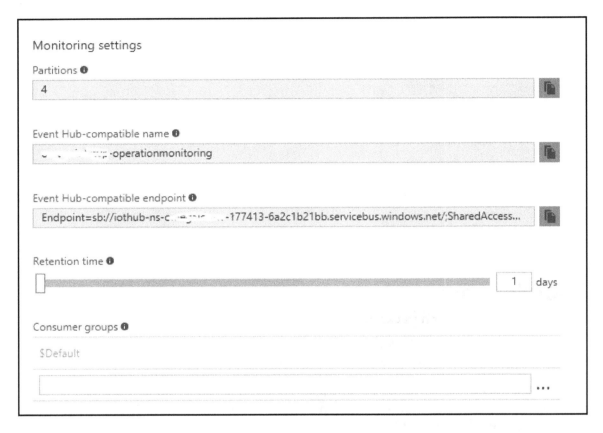

We can parse these events in the event processor host and send email alerts, or we can even connect with stream analytics and use the Power BI dashboard to see the operation monitoring in real-time.

The diagnostic metrics of the Azure IoT Hub

The Azure IoT Hub metrics maintain and give insights the overall IoT services, devices, communications, and more. These are very informative metrics in case you require Azure's support to drill down to any root cause of your IoT solution.

How to do it...

Lets use the **Metrics** of IoT Hub:

1. Log in to the Azure portal and navigate to the IoT Hub service.
2. Select the IoT Hub for which you want to view the metrics:

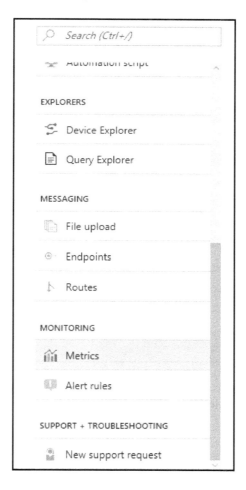

3. Select the metric from the available list:

4. This dashboard view for the selected metrics will be provided. You can filter for the chart type or period for which you want to look back into the data:

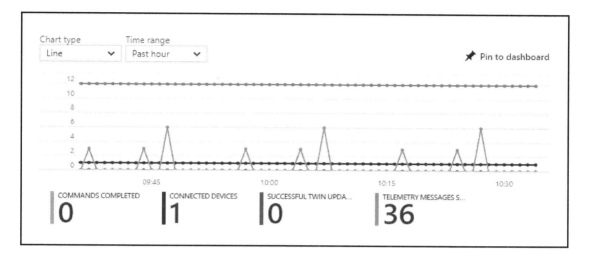

5. If any alerts are configured, you can see the alerts raised:

Scaling your IoT Hub solution

When rapid expansion in less time is the need for a business, a truly scalable system helps to grow the company by rolling out updates as needed, at a time or speed that helps the organization. Microsoft Azure provides scalability for all services, and it is also implemented with the IoT Hub. The need for scalability depends upon the performance characteristics that your IoT solution needs. A single IoT Hub unit can connect with millions of IoT devices. But based on the need, we can define more IoT Hub units and scale the solutions.

Getting ready

In this recipe, we will look for ways of scaling your IoT solutions, which you can implement after you identify their needs.

How to do it...

Lets scale the IoT Hub:

1. Log in to the Azure portal and navigate to the IoT Hub service.
2. Select the IoT Hub that you want to scale:

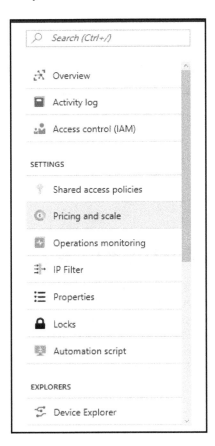

3. Select the pricing tier, which is sufficient for your IoT solution to scale vertically:

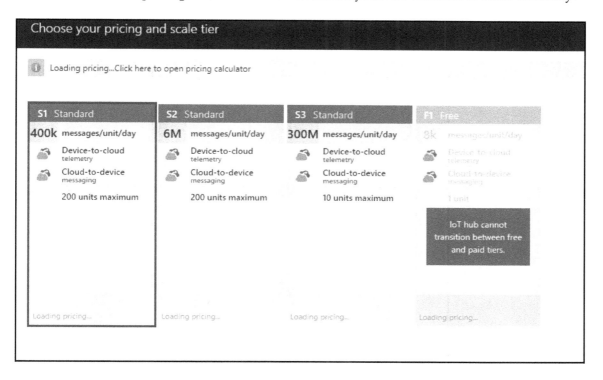

4. You can change the IoT Hub units to scale horizontally by using different instance sizes:

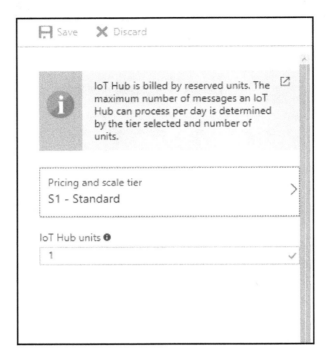

There's more...

Typically, the size of the IoT Hub is decided by the number of messages that are being sent by the IoT devices in one day.

Here is an IoT Hub instance size table:

Tier	Sustained throughput	Sustained send rate
S1	Up to 1111 KB/minute per unit (1.5 GB/day/unit)	Average of 278 messages/minute per unit (400,000 messages/day per unit)
S2	Up to 16 MB/minute per unit (22.8 GB/day/unit)	Average of 4167 messages/minute per unit (6 million messages/day per unit)
S3	Up to 814 MB/minute per unit (1144.4 GB/day/unit)	Average of 208,333 messages/minute per unit (300 million messages/day per unit)

Now let's take an example of how we are supposed to think about calculating the required IoT Hub size based on our deployment of IoT devices.

Consider a scenario where there are 10,000 IoT devices, which send data every second. What tier should you use and how many units? You need to send 10,000 messages per second so three units of S3 will suffice. You can also take 142 units of S2 for the same performance and price.

While this sample calculation will give you an understanding of how we should select the IoT Hub size, this is a very important design step when you are working on a very large number of IoT device solutions. if at the time of designing the solution these points are not considered the result could be a throttling of messages sent to the IoT Hub.

Index

W

Windows IoT Core

www.ingramcontent.com/pod-product-compliance
Lightning Source LLC
Chambersburg PA
CBHW060539060326
40690CB00017B/3546